Barack Obama
vs.
Mitt Romney
On The Issues

**Jesse Gordon,
OnTheIssues.org**

Table of Contents

Romney vs. Obama on International Issues 109

Book reviews 143

Romney vs. Obama on VoteMatch:....................156

Romney vs. Obama
On the Issues

Governor Mitt Romney of Massachusetts and President Barack Obama agree on some issues and disagree on many others. This book outlines their stances on the issues, in a side-by-side manner for each issue, on many of controversial topics that they will face as President.

We gather the two candidates' issue stances from their political autobiographies; from debates in both the 2012 election season and past elections; from public speeches; from campaign websites; and from political analysis websites. All of the excerpts appear, with many additional issue stances, on our website, www.OnTheIssues.org.

Obama is unopposed for the 2012 Democratic nomination, so we focus on his presidential speeches, as well as materials from past campaigns. Romney ran unsuccessfully for President in 2008, but has been one of the frontrunners from the start of the 2012 race. Some pundits claim that the solution to the Great Recession requires a business perspective—in other words, that Romney's time has come. This book explores how Romney's and Obama's issue stances differ, so you can decide for yourself if the pundits are right.

The purpose of this book, and the mission of our website, is to inform voters about candidates' issue stances—what they believe about the issues, and what they have done to implement those beliefs. The mainstream media report on candidates' politics: who's ahead this week; who "won" the last debate; who has endorsed whom. We reject the "horse race politics" that dominates the mainstream media, and instead focus on what matters: Romney on the issues versus Obama on the issues.

—Jesse Gordon, Editor-in-Chief, jesse@OnTheIssues.org
January 2012

Dedication

To Michele, Abe & Janice

Acknowledgments

This book would not have been possible without the tireless efforts of the entire OnTheIssues team: Derek Camara, Janice Gordon, Michele Gordon, Peter Hoerr, Ram Lau, Adam Leighton, Jamie Leighton, Naomi Lichtenberg, Ogden Porter, Will Rico, Dan Teittinen, Irma Teittinen, and especially Kathleen Camara.

Romney vs. Obama on Domestic Issues

Domestic issues focus on joint state-federal jurisdiction or enforcement, including the following topics:

- **Crime:** including mandatory sentencing and the death penalty. Gov. Romney supports both on law-and-order grounds; President Obama opposes both on liberal grounds.

- **Gun Control:** Pres. Obama's prefers a "collective right" to gun ownership, with numerous exceptions and local restrictions; Gov. Romney acknowledges the individual right to gun ownership, but still with numerous exceptions and local restrictions.

- **Drugs:** including marijuana legalization and the War on Drugs. Romney's law enforcement-focused policy compares with Obama's hands-off attitude towards the topic of legalization.

- **Environment:** including pollution and EPA issues (and domestic energy issues; also see wider energy issues in the International Issues section). Obama demonstrates a progressive attitude of enforcing anti-pollution and pro-environment policies; Romney differs little on themes but only on details.

- **Technology and Infrastructure:** including high-tech Internet issues, as well as low-tech roads and bridges investment issues. Obama would like a Mars program; Romney is unenthused about a Moon program. Obama wants to invest directly in infrastructure; Romney relies on funding infrastructure investment by growing the economy.

- **Health Care:** including federal healthcare and ObamaCare issues; plus Medicare/Medicaid and state issues. The two candidates agree on healthcare reform; the differences between ObamaCare and RomneyCare will be a major focus of the election campaign.

Mitt Romney on Domestic Issues

Barack Obama on Domestic Issues

Romney on Alternative Sentencing

One Strike, You're Ours: lifetime GPS tracking

Governor Romney announced that he would propose a "One Strike, You're Ours" law for those convicted of preying on children using the Internet. Massachusetts Republican District Attorneys and Sheriffs support Governor Romney's proposal for stiff mandatory jail time to be followed by lifetime tracking by Global Positioning Satellite (GPS) for first-time offenders: "As Governor of Massachusetts, Mitt Romney was a strong defender of children. He led the effort to put photos of the state's most dangerous sex offenders on the Internet and made it easier to extend civil commitments for sex offenders.

As a candidate for president, Governor Romney is once-again demonstrating strong leadership in protecting our children. His 'One Strike, You're Ours' law is an important initiative to strengthen law enforcement and protect America's sons and daughters. We are proud to stand alongside Governor Romney in his campaign for our nation's highest office.

Source: Press Release, "Law Enforcement Officials," July 21, 2007

NOTE: "Three Strikes" laws mandate that criminal offenders are sentenced to life imprisonment upon their third criminal conviction. The term refers to the baseball rule, "Three Strikes and You're Out." Romney's term "One Strike" is intended to be a stricter version of Three Strikes.

Obama on Alternative Sentencing

Supports alternative sentencing and rehabilitation

Principles that Obama supports to address crime:

- Implement penalties other than incarceration for certain non-violent offenders.

- Increase state funds for programs which rehabilitate and educate inmates during and after their prison sentences.

- Provide funding for military-style "boot camps" for first-time juvenile felons.

Source: State Legislative National Political Awareness Test, July 2, 1998

Reduce recidivism by giving offenders a Second Chance

Obama co-sponsored the Recidivism Reduction and Second Chance Act, which expands provisions for adult and juvenile offender state and local reentry demonstration projects. Directs the Attorney General to award grants for:

- State and local reentry courts;

- Comprehensive and Continuous Offender Reentry Task Forces;

- Drug treatment services to incarcerated offenders;

- Mentoring services for reintegrating offenders into the community;

- prison-based family treatment programs for incarcerated parents of minor children; and

Source: Second Chance Act (S.1060/H.R.1593) S1060 on March 29, 2007

Romney on Death Penalty

Supports death penalty in heinous murders

Romney pushes for a death penalty law for murderers convicted of heinous first-degree homicides. "The ultimate penalty should be available in Massachusetts for criminals who commit the most egregious murders," Romney said.

Source: Campaign web site, www.romney2002.com, "Issues,"
Sept. 17, 2002

Favored stricter sentencing and death penalty

- Supported death penalty

- Wanted to abolish parole, limit probation, and end furloughs and release programs for violent or repeat offenders

- Favored mandatory sentencing and three strikes and you're out

- Supported restrictions on plea bargaining

- His crime prevention efforts also focused on instilling family values.

Source: Boston Globe review of 1994 campaign issues, March 21, 2002

Obama on Death Penalty

Battled legislatively against the death penalty

Obama's most significant contribution has been his legislative battles against the death penalty, and against in the criminal justice system. In Illinois, it's been a series of shocking exonerations of innocent people who are on death row. He was involved very intimately in drafting and passing legislation that requires the video taping of police interrogations and confessions in all capital cases. And he also was one of the co-sponsors of this very comprehensive reform or the death penalty system in Illinois, which many people say may trigger the retreat on the death penalty in many other states.

Source: Salim Muwakkil and Amy Goodman, Democracy Now,
Jul 15, 2004

Death penalty should be enforced fairly and with caution

I think that the death penalty is appropriate in certain circumstances. There are especially heinous crimes: terrorism, the harm of children. Obviously, we've had some problems in this state in the application of the death penalty. That's why a moratorium was put in place and that's why I was so proud to be one of the leaders in overhauling a death penalty system that was broken. We became the first in the nation requiring the video taping of capital interrogations and confessions. We have to have this ultimate sanction in certain circumstances where the whole community says "this is beyond the pale."

Source: Illinois Senate Debate #3: Barack Obama vs. Alan Keyes,
Oct 21, 2004

Romney on Gun Rights

Ok to ban lethal weapons that threaten police

Q: Are you still for the Brady Bill?

A: The Brady Bill has changed over time, and, of course, technology has changed over time. I would have supported the original assault weapon ban. I signed an assault weapon ban in Massachusetts governor because it provided for a relaxation of licensing requirements for gun owners in Massachusetts, which was a big plus. And so both the pro-gun and the anti-gun lobby came together with a bill, and I signed that. And if there is determined to be, from time to time, a weapon of such lethality that it poses a grave risk to our law enforcement personnel, that's something I would consider signing. There's nothing of that nature that's being proposed today in Washington. But I would look at weapons that pose extraordinary lethality.

We should check on the backgrounds of people who are trying to purchase guns. We also should keep weapons of unusual lethality from being on the street. And finally, we should go after people who use guns in the commission of crimes or illegally, but we should not interfere with the right of law-abiding citizens to own guns, for their own personal protection or hunting or any other lawful purpose. I support the work of the NRA. I'm a member of the NRA. But do we line up on every issue? No, we don't.

Source: Meet the Press: 2007 "Meet the Candidates" series,
Dec. 16, 2007

Obama on Gun Rights

Respect 2nd Amendment, but local gun bans ok

Q: You said recently, "I have no intention of taking away folks' guns." How do you justify supporting the D.C. handgun ban?

A: Because I think we have two conflicting traditions in this country. I think it's important for us to recognize that we've got a tradition of handgun ownership and gun ownership generally. And a lot of law-abiding citizens use it for hunting, for sportsmanship, and for protecting their families. We also have a violence on the streets that is the result of illegal handgun usage. And so I think there is nothing wrong with a community saying we are going to take those illegal handguns off the streets. And cracking down on the various loopholes that exist in terms of background checks for children, the mentally ill. We can have reasonable gun control measure that I think respect the Second Amendment and people's traditions.

Source: 2008 Politico pre-Potomac Primary interview, Feb. 11, 2008

Provide some common-sense enforcement on gun licensing

Q: In the state senate, you talked about licensing and registering gun owners. Would you do that as president?

A: I don't think that we can get that done. But what we can do is to provide just some common-sense enforcement. The efforts by law enforcement to obtain the information required to trace back guns that have been used in crimes to unscrupulous gun dealers. As president, I intend to make it happen.

Source: 2008 Democratic debate in Las Vegas, Jan. 15, 2008

Romney on Drugs in Society

Combat the ruthless narco-terrorists in Colombia

On the 197th anniversary of Colombia's independence, we honor the many contributions that Colombian-Americans have made to our country. We also express our abiding solidarity with the Colombian people, who are fighting to secure their country's future from leftist guerrillas and narco-terrorists who have thrived on terror, violence and corruption for too many years.

A safe and prosperous Western Hemisphere requires a strong and democratic Colombia. The US must continue to provide strong support for Colombia's efforts to combat the ruthless narco-terrorists that operate there. Our partnership with Colombia contributes to our security and our quality of life—sowing stability in a critical region and helping keep deadly drugs off our streets. We can and must consolidate the gains we have made in Colombia by strengthening the economic ties between our countries. The U.S. Congress must treat this vital ally with the respect Colombia deserves and move forward now with the free trade agreement.

Source: Press Release, "Colombia Independence Day," July 20, 2007

NOTE: The U.S. "partnership with Colombia" refers to the U.S. policy called "Plan Colombia." Under Plan Colombia, the U.S. provides international aid to the government of Colombia in exchange for aerial spraying of cocaine crops and other anti-narcotic activities.

Obama on Drugs in Society

Expand drug courts; help prisoners with substance abuse

THE PROBLEM

Disparities Continue to Plague Criminal Justice System: African Americans and Hispanics are more than twice as likely as whites to be searched & arrested when stopped by police. Disparities in drug sentencing laws, like the differential treatment of crack as opposed to powder cocaine, are unfair.

OBAMA'S PLAN

- *Expand Use of Drug Courts:* Obama will give first-time, non-violent offenders a chance to serve their sentence, where appropriate, in the type of drug rehabilitation programs that have proven to work better than a prison term in changing bad behavior.

- *Reduce Crime Recidivism by Providing Ex-Offender Support:* Obama will provide job training, substance abuse and mental health counseling to ex-offenders, so that they are successfully re-integrated into society.

- *Eliminate Sentencing Disparities:* The disparity between sentencing crack and powder-based cocaine is wrong and should be completely eliminated.

Source: Campaign booklet, "Blueprint for Change," p. 49, Feb. 2, 2008

Romney on Marijuana Legalization

Opposes legalization of
recreational or medical marijuana

The former Massachusetts governor opposes the legalization of recreational or medical marijuana, although he endorsed the use of synthetic pot. In his most recent book, *No Apology*, he attributes the legalization movement to "the passion and zeal of those members of the pleasure-seeking generation that never grew up."

Source: Tim Murphy in Mother Jones magazine, Apr. 20, 2011

NOTE: Medical marijuana is legal or partially legal in 18 states as of 2012: Alaska, Arizona, California, Colorado, District of Columbia, Hawaii, Maine, Maryland, Michigan, Montana, Nevada, New Jersey, New Mexico, Oregon, Rhode Island, Vermont, Virginia, and Washington. Medical marijuana is also legal in numerous foreign countries. Medical marijuana alleviates symptoms associated with glaucoma, cancer, HIV/AIDS, and numerous mental diseases.

Obama on Marijuana Legalization

Not first candidate to use drugs, but first honest about it

One issue that exposed the disconnect between Obama's appeal & the conventional wisdom of an older generation is his drug use. The Washington Post focused on his use of drugs as a teen that he reveals in his book, Dreams from My Father: "Pot had helped, and booze; maybe a little blow when you could afford it. Not smack though."

Obama's honesty in addressing the issue reflects a generational change in politics. Most voters no longer care about youthful drug use; they're worried about having an honest person in the White House. In 1992, Bill Clinton answered a question about his drug use by saying he had tried marijuana, but "didn't inhale." When asked, "Did you inhale?" Obama replied, "That was the point." Obama was making fun of old-style politician who thought they could fool the voterObama is almost certainly isn't the first person to use cocaine and then run for president. But he is the first presidential candidate honest enough to talk about the troubles of his youth.

Source: The Improbable Quest, by John Wilson, pp. 12-3, Oct. 30, 2007

Romney on Nuclear Waste

Compensate Nevada for nuclear waste in Yucca Mountain

Q: [to Paul]: Do you support opening the national nuclear repository at Yucca Mountain?

PAUL: I've opposed this. I approach it from a state's rights position. What right does 49 states have to punish one state and say, "We're going to put our garbage in your state"?

ROMNEY: I don't always agree with Rep. Paul, but I do on that. The idea that 49 states can tell Nevada, "We want to give you our nuclear waste," doesn't make a lot of sense. I think the people of Nevada ought to have the final say as to whether they want that, and my guess is that for them to say yes, someone's going to have to offer them a pretty good deal, as opposed to having the federal government jam it down their throat. And if Nevada says, "Look, we don't want it," then let other states make bids and say, hey, look, we'll take it; here's the compensation we want for taking it. Let the free market work. And where the people say the deal's a good one will decide where we put this stuff.

Source: Primary debate in Las Vegas, Oct. 18, 2011

NOTE: Yucca Mountain is a federally-owned mountain in Nevada which the federal government has proposed as a long-term repository for nuclear waste. Yucca Mountain was selected because, in theory, it is geologically stable enough to survive intact for the thousands of years until the nuclear waste becomes harmless. The site was first proposed under Pres. Reagan in 1985-1987; Congress approved it under Pres. Bush in 2002; and then Congress canceled the program under Pres. Obama in April 2011.

Obama on Nuclear Waste

GovWatch: Opposes Yucca Mountain for nuclear waste storage

McCain portrays Obama as saying "no to clean, safe, nuclear energy." That's false. But there's no question that McCain is a much bigger advocate of nuclear power than Obama, who has taken a more guarded position. McCain has said that he'd work to bring 45 new nuclear power plants online by 2030, with the eventual goal of building 100 new nuclear plants. Obama has criticized that, highlighting his opposition to long-term storage of nuclear waste at the federal government's Yucca Mountain site in Nevada. "He wants to build 45 new nuclear reactors when they don't have a plan to store the waste anywhere besides right here," Obama said on June 25. McCain supports going ahead with the Yucca Mountain plan.

Obama's 2007 plan promised that he "will also lead federal efforts to look for a safe, long-term disposal solution based on objective, scientific analysis." It's inaccurate to cast Obama as an opponent, and McCain goes too far when he portrays Obama as saying "no" to nuclear.

Source: GovWatch on 2008: Washington Post analysis, June 26, 2008

Romney on Environmental Philosophy

Clean environment will be a campaign theme

Seizing on the momentum of his successful leadership of the Olympics in Salt Lake City, Romney revealed a campaign theme that relies heavily on his management and leadership experience.

"There have been too many left behind," Romney said after his announcement, in response to reporters' questions. "Our schools aren't solid enough; our environment has not been cleaned the way it could be. Our streets are not as safe as they could be. All these things could be made better in my view with the application of new leadership and sound management principles."

The millionaire venture capitalist said voters should not have trouble connecting with his candidacy. "Everything I've done over the last three years, I think, makes it clear that I'm very much connected with the people of our country and the people of our world," he said.

Source: Stephanie Ebbert, Boston Globe, p. B6, Mar. 20, 2002

Obama on Environmental Philosophy

Genesis teaches stewardship of earth: sacrifice for future

Q: Could you give an example of how you relate your faith to science policy?

A: One of the things I draw from the Genesis story is the importance of us being good stewards of the land, of this incredible gift. And I think there have been times where we haven't been [good stewards], and this is one of those times where we've got to take the warning seriously [about climate change]. And part of what my religious faith teaches me is to take an intergenerational view, to recognize that we are borrowing this planet from our children and our grandchildren. And this is where religious faith and the science of global warming converge: We have to find resources in ourselves to make sacrifices so we don't leave it to the next generation. We've got to be less wasteful, both as a society and in our own individual lives. I think religion can actually bolster our desire to make those sacrifices now. As president, I hope to rally the entire world around the importance of us being good stewards of the land.

Source: Democratic Compassion Forum at Messiah College, April 13, 2008

Romney on Emissions Standards

States should be able to have their own emissions standards

Q: Gov. Schwarzenegger has proposed that California be allowed to implement much tougher environmental regulations on emission requirements than apply to the rest of the country. Do you side with the governor or with the Bush administration?

A: I side with states to be able to make their own regulations with regards to emissions within their own states. I side with states being able to make their own decisions, even if I don't always agree with the decisions they make.

Source: 2008 Republican debate at Reagan Library in Simi Valley,
Jan. 30, 2008

Obama on Emissions Standards

Let states define stricter-than-federal emission standards

Obama co-sponsored a bill: To permit California and other States to effectively control greenhouse gas emissions from motor vehicles, and for other purposes. Amends the Clean Air Act to approve the application of the state of California for a waiver of federal preemption of its motor vehicle emission standards.

Source: Reducing Global Warming from Vehicles Act (S.2555 & H.R.5560) on Jan. 24, 2008

Include clean coal in clean energy future

Obama's plan to invest in a clean energy future and in renewable and alternative energies states that he will:

- *Invest $150 billion over ten years in clean energy:* Obama will advance the next generation of biofuels & fuel infrastructure, invest in low-emission coal plants, and begin the transition to a new digital electricity grid.

- *Develop and deploy clean coal:* Commercialize and deploy low-carbon coal technologies.

- *Deploy cellulosic ethanol:* Obama will invest federal resources, including tax incentives, cash prizes, & government contracts into developing the first 2 billion gallons of cellulosic ethanol into the system by 2013.

Source: Obamanomics, by John R. Talbott, pp.132-3, July 1, 2008

Romney on Energy Efficient Cars

$20 billion package for energy research & new car technology

Q: You pledged to offer a $20 billion package to help out the auto industry with energy research and new technology. One conservative columnist wrote, "Is that what a Republican should do, bail out a private industry?" Are you going to offer billions of taxpayer dollars to every industry that's in trouble in this country?

A: We spend about $4 billion a year right now on energy research to try and help us become less energy dependent on foreign sources. And I think over the coming years we need to increase our investment to become energy independent from about $4 billion a year to about $20 billion a year. Obviously, that has got to grow gradually because there are not a lot of places now that do the kind of research we need to do to get ourselves energy independent. But that's not just to bail out the automobile industry. That's not what I have in mind. I'm not looking for a bailout at all. Instead, it's saying that where we invest, we tend to do very well.

Source: 2008 Fox News interview: "Choosing the President" series,
Jan. 20, 2008

Obama on Energy Efficient Cars

Let's build a fuel-efficient car in America, not abroad

Q: Can we reduce our dependence on foreign oil and by how much in the first term, in four years?

OBAMA: We can't drill our way out of the problem. That's why I've focused on putting resources into solar, wind, biodiesel, geothermal. It is absolutely critical that we develop a high fuel efficient car that's built not in Japan and not in South Korea, but built here in the USA. We invented the auto industry and the fact that we have fallen so far behind is something that we have to work on.

Source: Third presidential debate against John McCain, Oct. 15, 2008

Romney on Infrastructure Investment

Invest in infrastructure from growing economy by lower taxes

Q: Do you want to raise taxes to fix more bridges? Or can we cut taxes to fix more bridges?

A: There's no question—if you really want to make some money in this country, really get some money so we can repair our infrastructure and build for the future, the biggest source of that is a growing American economy. If the economy is growing slowly, when tax revenues hardly move at all, and, boy, you better raise taxes to get more money for all the things you want to do. But if the economy is growing quickly, then we generate all sorts of new revenue. And the best way to keep the economy rolling is to keep our taxes down. Our bridges—let me tell you what we did in our state. We found that we had 500 bridges, roughly, that were deemed structurally deficient. And so we changed how we focused our money. Instead of spending it to build new projects—the bridge to nowhere, new trophies for congressmen—we instead said, "Fix it first." We have to reorient how we spend our money.

Source: 2007 GOP Iowa Straw Poll debate, Aug. 5, 2007

Obama on Infrastructure Investment

National Infrastructure Reinvestment Bank: $60 billion in 10 years

If we want to keep up with China or Europe, we can't settle for crumbling roads and bridges, aging water and sewer pipes, and faltering electrical grids that cost us billions to blackouts, repairs and travel delays. It's gotten so bad that the American Society of Civil Engineers gave our national infrastructure a "D." A century ago, Teddy Roosevelt called together leaders from business and government to develop a plan for 20th century infrastructure. It falls to us to do the same.

As President, I will launch a National Infrastructure Reinvestment Bank that will invest $60 billion over ten years—a bank that can leverage private investment in infrastructure improvements, and create nearly two million new jobs. The work will be determined by what will maximize our safety and security and ability to compete. We will fund this bank as we bring the war in Iraq to a responsible close. We can modernize our power grid, which will help conservation and spur on the development and distribution of clean energy

Source: Speech in Flint, MI, in Change We Can Believe In, p.255,
Jun 15, 2008

Romney on Outer Space Policy

Mining the moon costs too much

ROMNEY: Speaker Gingrich and I have a lot of places where we disagree.

Q: Why don't you name them?

ROMNEY: We can start with his idea to have a lunar colony that would mine minerals from the moon, I'm not in favor of spending that kind of money to do that.

GINGRICH: I'm proud of trying to find things that give young people a reason to study science and math and technology and telling them that someday in their lifetime, they could dream of going to the moon, they could dream of going to Mars. I grew up in a generation where the space program was real, where it was important, and where frankly it is tragic that NASA has been so bureaucratized. Iowa's doing brilliant things, attracting brilliant students. I want to give them places to go and things to do. And I'm happy to defend the idea that America should be in space and should be there in an aggressive, entrepreneurial way.

Source: Yahoo's "Your Voice Your Vote" debate in Iowa,
Dec. 10, 2011

Obama on Outer Space Policy

Cancel moon program; develop human mission to Mars

Obama wants to end NASA's moon program, turn over space transportation to commercial companies and jump-start technologies needed for future human exploration of Mars.

NASA has been working to develop a replacement for the space shuttles, which are being retired this year after five more missions to complete construction of the orbiting International Space Station, a $100 billion project of 16 nations.

Obama's budget ends work on the shuttle follow-on vehicle, known as Orion, as well as a pair of rockets developed to fly astronauts to the space station, the moon and other destinations in the solar system.

"We are proposing canceling the program, not delaying it," said a spokesperson. Funds previously earmarked for the Constellation program, initially intended to return US astronauts to the moon by 2020, instead would be used for research projects that include robotics and other technologies needed to prepare for an eventual human mission to Mars.

Source: Reuters wire service, "Obama axes NASA moon plan,"
Jan. 31, 2010

Romney on R&D Spending

National R&D spending OK; picking winners not OK

Government funding for basic science and research in universities and research laboratories has been declining for years. It needs to grow instead, particularly in engineering and the physical sciences. Research in energy, materials science, nanotechnology, and transportation are vital to the economy and to our nation's competitiveness. Government should not, however, attempt to pick winning ideas or technologies in which it would invest funds for development and commercialization.

The realities of that marketplace sort out those that have potential for growth and sustainability and those that do not. Attempting to substitute government for the roles carried out by entrepreneurs, angel investors, and venture capitalists while also bypassing the unforgiving test of the free market is a very bad idea indeed.

Source: No Apology, by Mitt Romney, pp.124-5, March 2, 2010

Obama on R&D Spending

Space-race-level investment in R&D; biotech; & green tech

We know what it takes to compete for the jobs and industries of our time. We need to out-innovate, out-educate, and out-build the rest of the world. The first step in winning the future is encouraging American innovation.

Our free enterprise system is what drives innovation. But because it's not always profitable for companies to invest in basic research, throughout our history, our government has provided cutting-edge scientists and inventors with the support that they need.

This is our generation's Sputnik moment. Two years ago, I said that we needed to reach a level of research and development we haven't seen since the height of the Space Race. I will be sending a budget to Congress that helps us meet that goal. We'll invest in biomedical research, information technology, and especially clean energy technology—an investment that will strengthen our security, protect our planet, and create countless new jobs for our people.

Source: FactCheck.org on 2011 State of the Union speech, Jan. 26, 2011

Romney on Health Mandate

Personal responsibility instead of employer mandates

Q: What should we do with all the millions of people who are not insured?

A: Well, I actually got the job done. Working with people across the aisle, we said: Enough is enough. Look, the best kind of prevention you can have in health care is to have a doctor. And if someone doesn't have a doctor, doesn't have a clinic they can go to, doesn't have health insurance to be able to provide the prescription drugs they need, you can't be healthy. And you need to have health insurance for all of our citizens.

And I found a way to do that without requiring raising taxes, without a government mandate, without a government takeover. When I said government mandate, I meant employer mandate. Instead, we have personal responsibility. We allowed individuals to buy their own policies. Those that couldn't afford them, we helped them buy their policies. And you know what? It cost us no more money to help people buy insurance policies that they could afford than it was costing us before, handing out free care.

Source: Republican primary debate on Univision, Dec. 9, 2007

Obama on Health Mandate

Zero fines & no mandate for small business

McCAIN: Sen. Obama wants, if you've got [a small business with] employees, if you don't adopt the health care plan that Sen. Obama mandates, he's going to fine you. Now, Sen. Obama, I'd still like to know what that fine is going to be.

OBAMA: Here's your fine—zero. Zero, because as I said in our last debate and I'll repeat, I exempt small businesses from the requirement for large businesses that can afford to provide health care to their employees, but are not doing it. I exempt small businesses from having to pay into a kitty. But large businesses that can afford it, we've got a choice. Either they provide health insurance to their employees or somebody has to. Right now, what happens is those employees get dumped into either the Medicaid system, which taxpayers pick up, or they're going to the emergency room for uncompensated care, which everybody picks up in their premiums.

Source: Third presidential debate against John McCain, Oct. 15, 2008

Voluntary universal participation, like in Medicare Part B

I believe that if we make [health insurance] affordable, people will purchase it. In fact, Medicare Part B is not mandated, it is voluntary. And yet people over 65 choose to purchase it, because it's a good deal. And if people end up seeing a plan that is affordable for them, I promise you they are snatching it up because they are desperate to get health care.

Source: Democratic Debate in Cleveland, Feb. 26, 2008

Romney on Medicare

Reform Medicare, but don't cancel prescription program

Q: [to Perry]: If you were president, would you repeal prescription drug benefits for seniors under Medicare?

PERRY: No. But it's a $17 trillion hole that we have in our budget we've got to deal with.

Q: [to Romney] How about you?

ROMNEY: I wouldn't repeal it. I'd reform Medicare and reform Medicaid and reform Social Security to get them on a sustainable basis, not for current retirees, but for those in their 20s and 30s and early 50s.

Source: Tea Party debate in Tampa FL, Sept. 12, 2011

Get everybody insured with state-based market dynamics

The way we improve something is not by putting more government into it. In my view, instead, the right way for us to go is to bring in place the kind of market dynamics that make the rest of the economy so successful. So my plan gets everybody in America insured, takes the burden of free riders off of our auto companies and everybody else, and says let's get everybody in the system.

Instead of having the federal government give you government insurance, Medicare and federal employee insurance, let's have private insurance.

Source: Republican debate in Dearborn, Michigan, Oct. 9, 2007

Obama on Medicare

Medicare is major driver of our long-term liabilities

Pres. OBAMA: The major driver of our long-term liabilities, is Medicare and Medicaid and our health care spending. That's going to be what our children have to worry about. Now, [Rep. Paul Ryan's] approach—if I understand it correctly, would say we're going to provide vouchers of some sort for current Medicare recipients at the current level.

Rep. RYAN: No.

Pres. OBAMA: No?

Rep. RYAN: People 55 and above are grandfathered in.

Pres. OBAMA: But just for future beneficiaries, the basic idea would be that at some point we hold Medicare cost per recipient constant as a way of making sure that that doesn't go way out of whack, right?

Rep. RYAN: We drew it as a blend of inflation and health inflation. Medicare is a $38 trillion unfunded liability—it has to be reformed for younger generations because it's going bankrupt. And the premise of our idea is, why not give people the same kind of health care plan we here have in Congress?

Source: Obama Q&A at House Republican retreat, Jan. 29, 2010

Romney on ObamaCare

I stand by what I did in Massachusetts; but not ObamaCare

Q: Do you stand by what you did with the health care mandate in Massachusetts?

ROMNEY: Absolutely. I'm not running for governor. I'm running for president. And if I'm president, on day one I'll direct the secretary of Health and Human Services to grant a waiver from Obamacare to all 50 states. It's a problem that's bad law, it's not constitutional. I'll get rid of it.

Q: [to Perry]: Can a state like Massachusetts go ahead and pass health care reform, including mandates? Is that a good idea, if Massachusetts wants to do it?

PERRY: Well, that's what Gov. Romney wanted to do, so that's fine. But the fact of the matter is, that was the plan that President Obama has said himself was the model for Obamacare. I don't think it was right for Massachusetts when you look at what it's costing the people of Massachusetts today.

ROMNEY: If you think what we did in Massachusetts and what Pres. Obama did are the same, boy, take a closer look: he raised taxes $500 billion; we didn't raise taxes.

Source: Tea Party debate in Tampa FL, Sept. 12, 2011

Obama on ObamaCare

Repealing healthcare reform would cost $250B

The only way to tackle our deficit is to cut excessive spending wherever we find it. This means further reducing health care costs, including programs like Medicare and Medicaid, which are the single biggest contributor to our long-term deficit. The health insurance law we passed last year will slow these rising costs, which is part of the reason that nonpartisan economists have said that repealing the health care law would add a quarter of a trillion dollars to our deficit. Still, I'm willing to look at other ideas to bring down costs, including one that Republicans suggested last year—medical malpractice reform to rein in frivolous lawsuits.

Source: State of the Union speech, Jan. 26, 2011

FactCheck: ObamaCare saves $2B to $10B, not $250B

Many of the cost-saving measures the president has touted are untested, such as changes in the way care is delivered, new payment models and pilot projects that some experts applaud, and others question.

The nonpartisan Congressional Budget Office expects that for most Americans, who get their insurance through work, health insurance premium costs won't change significantly from what they would have been without the law. CBO estimated that the major parts will cost $10 billion over the 2010-2019 period, while Medicare's Office of the Actuary determined savings of only $2 billion.

Source: FactCheck.org on State of the Union speech, Jan. 26, 2011

Romney vs. Obama on Economic Issues

Economic issues focus on the recession recovery and all fiscal matters, including the following topics:

- *Budget & Economy:* including deficit spending and all aspects of the federal budget. Gov. Romney opposes all bailouts and economic stimulus. Obama focuses instead on how to distribute the economic stimulus more fairly.

- *Corporations:* including corporate taxation and corporate welfare. Obama would raise corporate taxes and taxes on high-income earners. Romney would reduce both; but the campaign will focus on Romney's personal history as a corporate leader (or as a "vulture capitalist," depending on one's point of view).

- *Government Reform:* focusing on the size and role of the federal government, which Romney thinks should be smaller and more restricted. The two candidates most strongly disagree on campaign finance: Romney wants unlimited donations; Obama wants public funding.

- *Jobs:* including unemployment and union issues. Romney would restrict unions and limit unemployment compensation; Pres. Obama supports the opposite on both issues.

- *Social Security:* including the current Trust Fund and changes for the future. Gov. Romney would provide opt-out mechanisms; Pres. Obama opposes any form of privatization.

- *Tax Reform:* including income taxes, tax rates, and bracket redistribution. Romney would radically reduce taxes, citing supply-side economics for corporate tax reductions, but focusing on the middle class for income tax reductions. Pres. Obama focuses on revenue enhancement for fairness and for fixing the economy.

Mitt Romney
on Economic Issues

Barack Obama
on Economic Issues

Romney on Corporation Policy

Corporations are people

Campaigning in Iowa, Mitt Romney told a heckler, "Corporations are people, my friend"—words immediately seized upon by Democrats in what they termed as a possible defining statement by the presidential candidate.

Romney, speaking to a crowd at the Iowa State Fair, was being pressed about raising taxes to help cover entitlement spending. When one mentioned raising corporate tax rates, Romney responded by saying corporations were no different than people. The line earned him a sustained round of applause from the crowd.

But the Democratic National Committee fired off emails almost immediately after the remarks, as part of a continuing effort to frame the GOP frontrunner as an out-of-touch elitist, writing: "This is what Mitt Romney is going to run on?

A small band of hecklers, positioned near the stage, continually quarreled with Romney about whether wealthy Americans should pay higher taxes. "There was a time in this country when we didn't attack people based on their success," Romney said.

Source: James Oliphant in the Los Angeles Times, Aug. 11, 2011

Obama on Corporation Policy

I will raise CEO taxes, no doubt about it

Q: McCain is going to say you're going to raise taxes.

A: I will raise CEO taxes. There is no doubt about it.

Q: What about the average American?

A: If you are a CEO in this country, you will probably pay more taxes. They won't be prohibitively high. You're going to be paying roughly what you paid in the '90s, when CEOs were doing just fine.

Q: So, you want to just eliminate the Bush tax cuts?

A: I want to eliminate the Bush tax cuts. And what I have said is, I will institute a middle-class tax cut. So, if you're making $75,000, if you're making $50,000 a year, you will see an extra $1,000 a year offsetting on your payroll tax.

Q: Define middle class.

A: Well, look, I think that the definitions are always a little bit rough, but if you're making $100,000 a year or less, then you're pretty solidly middle class, and you deserve relief right now, as opposed to paying higher taxes. But people who are making over $200,000 or $250,000 have benefited the most from economic growth.

Source: CNN Late Edition: 2008 presidential series with Wolf Blitzer,
May 11, 2008

Romney on Financial Bailout

Bailout program wasted money;
let companies go bankrupt

Q: GM and Chrysler have rebounded. Would you say the bailout program was a success?

A: The bailout program was not a success because it wasted $17 billion. When the auto company CEOs went to Washington asking for money, I said the right process is not big check from Washington, but instead letting these enterprises go through bankruptcy, getting rid of the unnecessary costs, and re-emerge on their feet again. Instead, the Bush administration and the Obama administration wrote checks to the auto industry.

Q: You wrote in Nov. 2008, "If GM, Ford and Chrysler get the bailout, you can kiss the American automotive industry goodbye." Were you wrong?

A: No, I wasn't wrong, because if you read the rest of the op-ed piece, it says they need to shed unnecessary costs. If they just get federal checks, they're going to be locked in with high UAW legacy costs. They'll never be able to get on their feet. They have to go through bankruptcy. And it turned out that that's finally what they did.

Source: GOP primary debate in Manchester NH, June 13, 2011

Obama on Financial Bailout

We all hated the bank bailout; but it was necessary

Our most urgent task upon taking office was to shore up the same banks that helped cause this crisis. It was not easy to do. And if there's one thing that has unified Democrats and Republicans, and everybody in between, it's that we all hated the bank bailout. I hated it. You hated it. It was about as popular as a root canal.

But when I ran for President, I promised I wouldn't just do what was popular—I would do what was necessary. And if we had allowed the meltdown of the financial system, unemployment might be double what it is today.

So I supported the last administration's efforts to create the financial rescue program. And when we took that program over, we made it more transparent and more accountable. And as a result, the markets are now stabilized, and we've recovered most of the money we spent on the banks. Most but not all.

To recover the rest, I've proposed a fee on the biggest banks. I am not interested in punishing banks. I'm interested in protecting our economy.

Source: State of the Union Address, Jan. 27, 2010

Romney on Wall Street Reform

I was CEO at mainstream businesses, not Wall St.

CAIN: Gov. Romney has a very distinguished career. There's one difference between the two of us in terms of our experience. With all due respect, his business executive experience has been more Wall Street-oriented; mine has been more Main Street. I have managed small companies. I've actually had to clean the parking lot. I've worked with groups of businesses.

ROMNEY: The fact that we're both doing as well as we are is we both have a private-sector background. But I just want to set the record straight. I've been chief executive officer four times, once for a start-up and three times for turnarounds. One was a financial services company. That was the start-up. A consulting company, that's a mainstream business. The Olympics, that's certainly mainstream. And, of course, the state of Massachusetts. In all those settings, I've learned how to create jobs.

Source: Primary debate in Las Vegas, Oct. 18, 2011

Obama on Wall Street Reform

Pay attention to Main Street, not just Wall Street

OBAMA: Unless we are holding ourselves accountable day-in, day-out, not just when there's a crisis for folks who have power and influence and can hire lobbyists but for the nurse, the teacher, the police officer who frankly at the end of each month, they've got a little financial crisis going on. They're having to take out extra debt just to make their mortgage payments. We haven't been paying attention to them.

McCAIN: We've got fundamental problems in the system. And Main Street is paying a penalty for the excesses and greed in Washington and on Wall Street. We have a long way to go.

Q: Are you going to vote for the Senate bailout plan?

McCAIN: Sure. But there's also the issue of responsibility. I've been criticized for calling for the resignation of the SEC chairman. We've got to start also holding people accountable.

OBAMA: McCain's absolutely right that we need more responsibility, but we need it not just when there is a crisis. We've had years in which the reigning economic ideology has been what's good for Wall Street but not what's good for Main Street. There are folks out there who have been struggling before this crisis took place. And that's why it's so important we look at some of the underlying issues that have led to wages and incomes for ordinary Americans to go down, a health care system that is broken, energy policies that are not working. Unless we are holding ourselves accountable day-in, day-out, not just when there's a crisis for folks who have power and influence and can hire lobbyists.

Source: First presidential debate, Obama vs. McCain, Sept. 26, 2008

Romney on Economic Stimulus

Key to economic stimulus:
get companies to buy more stuff

Q: The president's economic stimulus plan would send out 116 million checks to American homes. The plan is somewhat contrary to yours, providing lots of short-term stimulus to individuals. Your plan focuses as much on the long term as the short term. Are you disappointed that your recipe for the economy was not embraced by the president? And will you now embrace his plan?

A: Well, there's a great deal that is effective in his plan. First, he's getting money back to consumers. That makes sense to me I just think we need to go further. We go to corporate support and helping corporations have the incentive to buy more capital equipment. That he also does. I do it more aggressively by writing off a larger amount of capital expenditures—getting companies to buy more stuff so that other companies will hire people. If you want to turn an economy around, the key thing is to grow jobs. It's not just to get checks in the hands of consumers; it's consumers & companies buying things that create jobs.

Source: GOP debate in Boca Raton Florida, Jan. 24, 2008

Obama on Economic Stimulus

$1 trillion avoided Depression;
but I took office with $8 trillion debt

Let me start the discussion of government spending by setting the record straight. At the beginning of the last decade, the year 2000, America had a budget surplus of over $200 billion. By the time I took office, we had a one-year deficit of over $1 trillion and projected deficits of $8 trillion over the next decade. Most of this was the result of not paying for two wars, two tax cuts, and an expensive prescription drug program. On top of that, the effects of the recession put a $3 trillion hole in our budget. All this was before I walked in the door.

Just stating the facts. Now, if we had taken office in ordinary times, I would have liked nothing more than to start bringing down the deficit. But we took office amid a crisis. And our efforts to prevent a second depression have added another $1 trillion to our national debt. That, too, is a fact. I'm absolutely convinced that was the right thing to do.

Source: State of the Union Address, Jan. 27, 2010

Romney on Trickle-Down Economics

Lowering taxes, like Bush tax cuts, grows the economy

Q: Would you explain why your record on taxes is better than your competitors?

ROMNEY: Lowering taxes grows the economy. Lowering taxes helps build jobs & helps working families, and so I strongly have been of the view that one of the great lessons for Ronald Reagan was that lowering taxes helped built our economy. Sen. McCain was one of two Republicans who voted against the Bush tax cuts. I believe the Bush tax cuts helped our economy grow and are one of the reasons that we're not in a recession today Senator McCain continues to believe that that was the right vote to take, and I respect that that's his view. I just happen to disagree with it. As governor, I fought tirelessly to reduce taxes. We cut taxes some 19 times in our state, and we held down s

Source: 2008 Fox News NH Republican primary debate, Jan. 6, 2008

Obama on Trickle-Down Economics

Not enough to help those at the top: it doesn't trickle down

Q: How can we bail people out of economic ruin?

OBAMA: It's not enough just to help those at the top. Prosperity is not just going to trickle down. We've got to help the middle class. Part of the problem is that for many of you, wages and incomes have flat-lined. For many of you, it is getting harder and harder to save, harder and harder to retire. Sen. McCain is right that we've got to stabilize housing prices. But underlying that is loss of jobs and loss of income. That's something that the next treasury secretary is going to have to work on.

McCAIN: We obviously have to stop this spending spree that's going on in Washington. Do you know that we've laid a $10 trillion debt on young Americans?

Source: Second presidential debate against John McCain, Oct. 7, 2008

Bottom-up economics instead of trickle-down economics

Obama explained that a healthy economy is a bottom-up economy, not a top-down economy dependent on trickle-down economics. In a bottom-up economy, the rules of business and government are fair and apply to all. There is a level playing field. Obama believes that all will benefit from the system he envisions, that Wall Street & Main Street are intertwined, that you can't have successful companies without motivated engaged workers

Source: Obamanomics, by John R. Talbott, pp. 18-9, July 1, 2008

Romney on National Debt

The "Party of No" is ok
when it comes to spending

The president accuses us of being the party of no. It's as if he thinks that by saying no, it's by definition a bad thing. In fact, it's right and praiseworthy to say no to bad things. It's right to say no to Cap-and-trade, no to Card Check, no to government healthcare, no to higher taxes.

Our party can never be a rubber stamp for rubber-stamp spending. But before we move away from this "No" epithet that the Democrats are fond of trying to apply to us, let's ask the Obama folks why they say no: no to a balanced budget, no to reforming entitlements, no to malpractice reform, no to missile defense in eastern Europe, no to tax cuts. You see, we conservatives don't have a corner on saying no. We're just the ones who say it when it's the right thing to say.

Source: Speech to 2010 Conservative Political Action Conference,
Feb. 20, 2010

Obama on National Debt

Freeze annual domestic spending for next five years

Now that the worst of the recession is over, we have to confront the fact that our government spends more than it takes in. That is not sustainable. Every day, families sacrifice to live within their means. They deserve a government that does the same.

This freeze will require painful cuts. Already, we've frozen the salaries of hardworking federal employees for the next two years. I've proposed cuts to things I care deeply about, like community action programs. The Secretary of Defense has also agreed to cut tens of billions of dollars in spending that he and his generals believe our military can do without.

Source: State of the Union speech, Jan. 26, 2011

Romney on Balanced Budget

Cap how much government can spend as a percentage of GDP

If you go back a few years to JFK's time, the government at all levels—federal, state and local—was consuming about 27% of the US. economy. Today it consumes about 37% of the US economy. It's on track to get to 40%. We cease at some point to be a free economy. And the idea of saying, we just want a little more, just give us some more tax revenue, we need that, that is the answer for America.

The answer is to cut federal spending. The answer is to cap how much the federal government can spend as a percentage of our economy and have a balanced budget amendment.

And the second part of the answer is to get our economy to grow, because the idea of just cutting and cutting and taxing more—I understand mathematically those things work, but nothing works as well as getting the economy going. Get Americans back to work. Get them paying taxes. Get corporations growing in America. And I'll tell you, these kinds of problems will disappear.

Source: GOP debate at Dartmouth College, NH, Oct. 11, 2011

Obama on Balanced Budget

Appoint bipartisan fiscal commission and re-establish PAYGO

We know that we've got a major fiscal challenge in reining in deficits that have been growing for a decade, and threaten our future. That's why I've proposed a three-year freeze in discretionary spending other than what we need for national security.

At this point, we know that the budget surpluses of the '90s occurred in part because of the pay-as-you-go law, which said that, well, you should pay as you go and live within our means, just like families do every day. 24 Republicans voted for that, and I appreciate it. And we were able to pass it in the Senate yesterday.

But the idea of a bipartisan fiscal commission to confront the deficits in the long term died in the Senate the other day. So I'm going to establish such a commission by executive order and I hope that you participate, fully and genuinely, in that effort, because if we're going to actually deal with our deficit and debt.

Source: Obama Q&A at 2010 House Republican retreat in Baltimore,
Jan. 29, 2010

NOTE: "PAYGO" refers to a "pay-as-you-go" policy, where all expenditures in a bill are explicitly paid for, instead of requiring borrowing. The Budget Enforcement Act of 1990 required all new spending bills to include how the spending would be balanced by revenue enhancements (taxes or fees) or other spending cuts. The PAYGO statute expired in 2002, but some congressional bills still describe offsets for new spending.

Romney on Campaign Finance Reform

McCain-Feingold hurt our party
and hurt the First Amendment

Q: Back in 2002, when McCain was campaigning for you when you were running for governor of Massachusetts, you said McCain "has always stood for reform and change, and he's always fought the good battle, no matter what the odds." Now you're saying in N.H. that McCain is not an agent of change. Why have you changed your opinion?

A: Oh, I still think he's a battler for change. He's just been there 27 years and hasn't been able to get the job done. He has brought some bills in place like McCain-Feingold, which hurt our party & I think hurt the First Amendment. He fought for immigration law, which I think was a terrible course, which said that all the illegal aliens that had come here illegally would be able to stay in this country forever. That was a mistake. Washington is broken. America is saying it loud and clear. You had in Iowa a number of experienced senators going up against folks that were new faces, governors, and the experienced senators lost.

Source: Fox News interview: "Choosing the President" series, Jan. 6, 2008

NOTE: "McCain-Feingold" refers to the Bipartisan Campaign Reform Act of 2002, also known as BCRA, named after its sponsors, Sen. John McCain (R, AZ) and Sen. Russ Feingold (D, WI). McCain-Feingold doubled the campaign donation limit from $1,000 per person to $2,000 per person ($2,500 in 2012), known as "hard money." The law banned "soft money" contributions to political parties, but later Supreme Court cases, particularly "Citizens United," allowed unlimited soft money for purposes of advertising for or against a candidate as long as there was no "coordination" with the campaign.

Obama on Campaign Finance Reform

Public campaign financing
with free television & radio time

Obama supports public financing of campaigns combined with free television and radio time as a way to reduce the influence of moneyed special interests. In February 2007, Obama proposed a plan that requires major party candidates to agree on a fundraising truce, return excess money from donors, and stay within the public financing system for the General Election.

Source: Campaign website, BarackObama.com, "Resource Flyers,"
Aug 26, 2007

No lobbyist money; no PAC money;
fund campaigns instead

I don't take money from federal lobbyists. I don't take money from PACs. In reducing special interest lobbying, I alone of the candidates here have actually taken away the power of lobbyists. A law I passed this year says to lobbyists, if you are taking money from anybody and putting it together and then giving it to a member of Congress, that has to be disclosed. Ultimately what I'd like to see is a system of public financing of campaigns, and I'm a cosponsor of the proposal.

Source: Democratic debate in Las Vegas, Jan. 15, 2008

Romney on Card Check

"Card check" is a massive imposition on worker freedom

The most naked pro-union power play in decades is the AFL-CIO demand to change the process by which a union enters a company's workplace.

The proposed statute, known as "card check" legislation, would represent a massive imposition on the freedom of workers to choose whether or not to become part of a union. Currently, the decision about unionization is made by a secret-ballot vote by the company's employees, but because unions haven't been winning a lot of elections, they want to change the rules.

Under the AFL-CIO plan, the union would collect pro-unionization signature cards from a majority of employees, cards that could be collected over an extended period of time and without the knowledge of the employer that an organizing effort is under way; thus, employees could be targeted and pressured, one by one.

This is a remarkable departure from the one of the prerequisites of any democracy—that of a secret ballot. It's easy to imagine how this system could lead to employee harassment and coercion.

Source: No Apology, by Mitt Romney, p.112-113, March 2, 2010

NOTE: "Card Check" refers to a unionization process where potential union members sign (or check off) a card indicating they would join the union. When a majority of workers have checked their cards, the union forms. Mitt Romney and most Republicans argue that Card Check inappropriately replaces a secret ballot process, and is inherently coercive.

Obama on Card Check

FactCheck: Yes, wants to limit secret balloting for unions

The Statement:

In a speech at Virginia Beach, McCain took on Obama's stance on unions: "Obama is planning to take away your right to vote by secret ballot in labor elections," he said.

The Facts:

McCain is referring to a plan supported by labor unions. Currently, workers must get at least 30% of their colleagues to sign an authorization form to ask for union representation—then hold a secret-ballot vote to finalize it. The change Obama supports, part of the Employee Free-Choice Act, would let a union be recognized by the National Labor Relations Board immediately after the majority signs the authorization. Supporters of the change say it would cut down on the ability of employers to pressure their workers to vote against a union.

The Verdict:

True. McCain accurately represents Obama's stance, although they disagree on the merits of the plan. Organized labor backs Obama's position, while business groups & some non-union workers support McCain's.

Source: CNN FactCheck on 2008 presidential race, Oct. 13, 2008

Romney on Unemployment

Replace jobless benefits with
unemployment savings accounts

Q: You've suggested replacing government jobless benefits with individual unemployment savings accounts. Jobless benefits for millions of Americans are about to expire; would you extend them?

A: Unemployment benefits, I think they've gone on a long, long time. But I would rather see a reform of our unemployment system, to allow people to have a personal account which they're able to draw from as opposed to having endless unemployment benefits. Let's reform the system, make the system work better by giving people responsibility for their own employment opportunities and having that account, rather than doling out year after year more money from an unemployment system.

Q: Would you sign a bill to extend unemployment insurance if you were president right now?

A: If I were president right now, I would go to Congress with a new system for unemployment, which would have specific accounts from which people could withdraw their own funds. And I would not put in place a continuation of the current plan

Source: Iowa Straw Poll debate in Ames Iowa, Aug. 11, 2011

Obama on Unemployment

$4,000 tax credit for companies
who hire unemployed workers

The purpose of the American Jobs Act is simple: to put more people back to work and more money in the pockets of those who are working. It will create more jobs for construction workers, more jobs for teachers, more jobs for veterans, and more jobs for the long-term unemployed. It will provide a tax break for companies who hire new workers, and it will cut payroll taxes in half for every working American and every small business. It will provide a jolt to an economy that has stalled, and give companies confidence that if they invest and hire, there will be customers for their products and services. You should pass this jobs plan right away.

Pass this jobs bill, and starting tomorrow, small businesses will get a tax cut if they hire new workers or raise workers' wages. Pass this jobs bill, and companies will get a $4,000 tax credit if they hire anyone who has spent more than six months looking for a job. We have to do more to help the long-term unemployed in their search for work.

Source: Pres. Obama's 2011 Jobs Speech, Sept. 8, 2011

Romney on Social Security Privatization

Favors private accounts; prepared to be entirely bold

Romney said he "was prepared to be entirely bold," in taking on the politically perilous issue of entitlement spending, "but I'm not prepared to cut benefits for low-income Americans." He said he favored private accounts and would consider tying Social Security benefits to prices rather than wages for higher income Americans.

Source: Bloomberg.com report on GOP primary debate in Orlando,
Oct. 21, 2007

Private accounts work better than extending retirement age

Currently, we're taking more money into Social Security that we actually send out. For people 20 and 30 and 40 years old, we have four major options for Social Security.

- The one Democrats want: raise taxes. It's the wrong way.

- The president said let's have private accounts and take that surplus money that's being gathered now in Social Security and put that into private accounts. That works.

- Other people said, well, extend the retirement age. That mathematically works. It's not as attractive.

- And the last is to index the Social Security benefits to something other than wages. But, in my view, that's the wrong way to go, other than for higher-income Americans. Let's consider indexing based on prices rather than wages.

Source: GOP primary debate in Orlando, Florida, Oct. 21, 2007

Obama on Social Security Privatization

What do we do with the losers of privatizing?

"What would the Ownership Society do with the losers (if Social Security were privatized)? Unless we're willing to see seniors starve on the streets, we're going to have to cover their retirement expenses one way or another—and since we don't know in advance which of us will be losers, it makes sense for all of us to chip into a pool that gives us at least some guaranteed income in our golden years. That doesn't mean we shouldn't encourage individuals to pursue higher-risk, higher-return investment strategies. They should. It just means that they should do so with savings other than those put into Social Security."

Thus, Obama sees the key underlying fallacy of privatization proposals. If we allow people to invest in riskier assets in the stock market, we will just have more losers who end up gambling with their retirement money and end up with nothing at retirement.

Source: Obamanomics, by John R. Talbott, p.161, July 1, 2008

Privatization puts retirement at whim of stock market

Q: Would you raise the cap for Social Security tax above the current level of the first $97,500 worth of income?

A: I think that lifting the [$97,500 income] cap is probably going to be the best option. My personal view is that lifting the cap is much preferable to the other options that are available. And we should reject things that will weaken the system, including privatization, which essentially is going to put people's retirement at the whim of the stock market.

Source: Democratic primary debate at Dartmouth College, Sept. 6, 2007

Romney on Trust Fund

Congress taking money from Trust Fund is criminal

PERRY: You said that if people did [what Social Security does] in the private sector it would be called criminal. That's in your book.

ROMNEY: Governor Perry, you've got to quote me correctly. You said it's criminal [as a Ponzi scheme]. What I said was congress taking money out of the Social Security trust fund is like criminal and that is and it's wrong.

Source: Tea Party debate in Tampa FL, Sept. 12, 2011

So-called "Trust Fund" has defrauded American people

A fiction that's often used to obscure the extent of the crisis is the so-called Social Security Trust Fund, which the American public is assured has a large positive balance. Yet it is not a fund in the conventional sense of the world. From the fund's inception, money collected from payroll taxes hasn't been "locked away," but rather has been used to pay benefits of current beneficiaries. There simply is no "fund" safely invested somewhere. There is no fund, and there is no silver bullet.

The American people have been effectively defrauded out of their Social Security. In 1982, the government raised Social Security taxes with the intention of creating a surplus that could be set aside in some fashion for the baby boomers when they retired. But for the last thirty years, the surplus has been spent, not on retirement security, but on regular budget items.

Source: No Apology, by Mitt Romney, p.157, March 2, 2010

Obama on Trust Fund

Must capture new revenue;
no new Social Security Commission

OBAMA: We're going to have to capture some revenue in order to stabilize the Social Security system. You can't get something for nothing. And if we care about Social Security, which I do, and if we are firm in our commitment to make sure that it's going to be there for the next generation, and not just for our generation, then we have an obligation to figure out how to stabilize the system. I think we should be honest in presenting our ideas in terms of how we're going to do that and not just say that we're going to form a commission and try to solve the problem some other way.

CLINTON: With all due respect, the last time we had a crisis in Social Security was 1983. President Reagan and Speaker Tip O'Neill came up with a commission. That was the best and smartest way, because you've got to get Republicans and Democrats together. That's what I will do.

OBAMA: That commission raised the retirement age, and also raised the payroll tax. So Sen. Clinton can't have it both ways.

Source: Philadelphia primary debate, on eve of PA primary, April 16, 2008

Romney on Entitlement Policy

Rein in the excessive growth in entitlement programs

Right now, federal spending is about 60% for entitlements: Social security, Medicare and Medicaid. That's growing like crazy. It will be 70% entitlements, plus interest, by the time of the next president's second term. Then the military is about 20% today. No one is talking about cutting the military, we ought to grow it. There's not enough in the 20% to go after if we don't go after the entitlement problem. We're going to rein in the excessive growth in those areas. We're not going to change the deal on seniors, but we're going to have to change the deal for 20 and 30 and 40-year-olds, or we're going to bankrupt our country.

Source: Republican debate at Reagan Library in Simi Valley, Jan. 30, 2008

Reform entitlements by negotiating behind closed doors

Romney says it's time to reform the two major entitlement programs: Social Security and Medicare. "It's really not possible for us to remain a superpower without restructuring our entitlements programs," Romney says. Romney says leaders from both political parties will have to come up with a solution in private. "Sitting down, quietly, behind closed doors and having a full and complete discussion of various ways to bring the costs down and to keep it from getting out of control," Romney says.

Source: Radio Iowa, "Romney: reform," by O.Kay Henderson, Aug 25, 2006

Obama on Entitlement Policy

Good health care and tax reform will save entitlements

Q: How should we fix Social Security and other entitlement programs?

OBAMA: If we get our tax policies right so that they're good for the middle class, if we reverse the policies of the last eight years that got us into this fix in the first place and that Sen. McCain supported, then we are going to be in a position to deal with Social Security and deal with Medicare, because we will have a health care plan that actually works for you, reduces spending and costs over the long term, and Social Security that is stable and solvent for all Americans and not just some.

McCAIN: What we have to do with Medicare is have the smartest people in America come together, come up with recommendations, and then, like the base-closing commission idea we had, then we should have Congress vote up or down.

Source: Second presidential debate against John McCain, Oct. 7, 2008

Romney on Tax-and-Spend Policies

Reduce the tax burden on middle-income families

I don't stay awake at night worrying about the taxes that rich people are paying. I'm concerned about the taxes that middle class families are paying. They're under a lot of pressure. Gasoline's expensive. Home heating oil, particularly in the Northeast, is very difficult for folks. Health care costs are going through the roof. Education costs and higher education are overwhelming. And as a result, we need to reduce the burden on middle-income families in this country.

Source: Des Moines Register Republican Debate, Dec. 12, 2007

I cut taxes 19 times as MA governor

Q: In 2005, you successfully appealed to upgrade your state's credit rating. You said you used a combination of spending cuts and new revenues to put Massachusetts on a more sound financial footing. You even approvingly cited a tax increase passed by the state legislature. Doesn't this show that sometimes raising taxes is necessary?

A: No. I don't believe in raising taxes. And as governor I cut taxes 19 times and didn't raise taxes. I was fortunate enough to be a governor that got an increase in the credit rating in my state. Republicans and Democrats worked together to cut spending. I came in, we had a huge deficit. We cut spending. Every single year I was governor we balanced the budget. That kind of leadership is what allowed us to get a credit upgrade from Standard & Poor's. And that's the leadership we finally need in the White House.

Source: Iowa Straw Poll GOP debate in Ames Iowa, Aug. 11, 2011

Obama on Tax-and-Spend Policies

We need a tax code where everybody pays their fair share

I'm well aware that there are many Republicans who don't believe we should raise taxes on those who are most fortunate and can best afford it. But here is what every American knows. While most people in this country struggle to make ends meet, a few of the most affluent citizens and corporations enjoy tax breaks and loopholes that nobody else gets. Right now, Warren Buffet pays a lower tax rate than his secretary—an outrage he has asked us to fix. We need a tax code where everyone gets a fair shake, and everybody pays their fair share.

Source: Pres. Obama's 2011 Jobs Speech, Sept. 8, 2011

2011 budget calls for top bracket of 39.6% to replace 35%

Right now, the top marginal tax rate is about 42% (35% federal, 2.9% Medicare, and an average of 4% of state and local income taxes). But Obama's tax plans will send our top marginal rate skyrocketing.

Obviously, Obama and Congress are going to push for increases on taxes for the wealthy. In his 2011 budget, Obama calls for going back to the pre-Bush top bracket of 39.6% from the current level of 35%.

Source: Take Back America, by Dick Morris, pp. 63-4, April 13, 2010

Romney on Death Tax

Death tax just doesn't make sense

- *Just say No:* "I said no to a tax hike; raising taxes hurts working people and scares away jobs. I also said no to more borrowing; borrowing just shifts our problems to the backs of our kids. Instead, I went after waste, inefficiency, duplication, and patronage."

- *The Death Tax:* "It doesn't make sense to me that people get taxed when they can earn their money, get taxed when they save their money, and get taxed when they die. We should get rid of the death tax.

Source: The Man, His Values, & His Vision, p.115, Aug. 31, 2007

Obama on Death Tax

2011 budget proposed to raise Death Tax to 45%

One likely candidate for an increase is the so-called Death Tax—the inheritance tax that has fallen to zero in 2010 due to the schedule of Bush tax cuts passed in 2001. In his 2011 budget, Obama proposes to hike the tax back up to 45% in 2011 and apply it to all estates worth more than $3.5 million. So, if you're planning to die soon, you'd better go to your Maker in 2010—while the tax is still at zero!

The problem with the Death Tax isn't how it affects families that own the wealth so much as how it impacts those who earn money to accumulate it. The tax itself is paid by only the top 2% of families. The central question for wealthy elderly Americans is what to do with their money. Should they keep it in cash or easily liquefied investments, or is it better to plow the money back into their businesses?

The Death Tax creates an incentive *not* to invest money in one's business, but to keep it in things like houses and yachts and luxury goods—or cash and gold and bonds—that are easier to liquidate.

Source: Take Back America, by Dick Morris, pp. 65-6, April 13, 2010

Romney vs. Obama on Social Issues

Social issues focus on matters which are based primarily on moral values, including the following topics:

- *Abortion:* including stem cells, partial birth, and state-level restrictions. This topic has always been the most viewed topic on our website www.OnTheIssues.org, so we explore several aspects. Romney is anti-stem-cell and pro-life, but makes numerous exceptions; Obama supports stem-cell research and abortion rights but it's not his major focus.

- *Civil Rights:* including gay rights and minority rights. For the 2012 race, gay rights will dominate this category. While Romney was governor of Massachusetts, his state's supreme court passed the nation's first same-sex marriage law. Romney is moderate on affirmative action. Obama moved gay rights forward and would like to move beyond race-based affirmative action.

- *Education:* including college funding issues, school vouchers, and school prayer. Romney and Obama both seek more college graduates; but disagree on how to get there. They also disagree on No Child Left Bind, and school vouchers.

- *Families and Children:* including father's rights and family values; not a key focus for either candidate.

- *Principles and Values:* including religious issues and party issues. We cite opinions on the Tea Party and personal religious faith, although both candidates deemphasize these topics.

- *Welfare and Poverty:* including homelessness, welfare payments, and other poverty programs. Romney wants to focus welfare on providing work opportunities; Obama wants to keep a more traditional approach.

Mitt Romney
on Social Issues

Barack Obama
on Social Issues

Romney on Partial-Birth Abortion

No punishment for women
who have partial birth abortions

Q: What would be the legal consequences to people who participated in illegal abortions?

A: They would be like the consequences associated with the bill relating to partial birth abortion which does not punish the woman. No one I know of is calling for punishing the woman. In the case of a doctor, the kinds of penalties would be potentially losing a license or having some other kind of restriction. In the case of partial birth abortion, as I recall, the penalty is a possible prison term not to exceed two years. But generally the medical profession would immediately follow the law. That's not going to be an issue. And there would be a recognition that one's license was at risk if one violated the law.

Source: Meet the Press: "Meet the Candidates" series, Dec. 16, 2007

Notes: "Partial-Birth Abortion" refers to a late-term abortion method which induces a breech delivery and collapses the fetal skull before completing delivery. This procedure is banned in 29 states, but pro-choice advocates, including former President Clinton, have sought to overturn state laws with a federal ruling.

- In June 2000, the Supreme Court rejected a Nebraska ban as unconstitutional because it had no exceptions and barred second trimester abortions.

- In Nov. 2003, Pres. Bush signed the Partial-Birth Abortion Ban Act; it was challenged in court by pro-choice groups.

- In April 2007, the Supreme Court upheld the ban, but allowed for future cases about how it is applied.

Obama on Partial-Birth Abortion

Trust women to make own decisions on partial-birth abortion

Q: What us your view on the decision on partial-birth abortion and your reaction to most of the public agreeing with the court's holding?

A: I think that most Americans recognize that this is a profoundly difficult issue for the women and families who make these decisions. They don't make them casually. And I trust women to make these decisions in conjunction with their doctors and their families and their clergy. And I think that's where most Americans are.

Now, when you describe a specific procedure that accounts for less than 1% of the abortions that take place, then naturally, people get concerned, and I think legitimately so. But the broader issue here is: Do women have the right to make these profoundly difficult decisions? And I trust them to do it.

There is a broader issue: Can we move past some of the debates around which we disagree and can we start talking about the things we do agree on? Reducing teen pregnancy; making it less likely for women to find themselves in these circumstances.

Source: South Carolina Democratic primary debate, on MSNBC,
Apr 26, 2007

Romney on Stem Cells

Stem cell research lofty goals
don't justify destroying life

Romney adopted the "pro-life" label after his battle over stem cell research. Ann Romney has multiple sclerosis. Romney, who not surprisingly cites the diagnosis of his wife's disease as one of the greatest blows of his life, is nevertheless alarmed by the aggressive program of embryonic stem cell research consortiums. He has taken a stand against the Harvard Stem Cell Institute.

The Harvard Stem Cell Institute was seeking legal protection for an embryo production line for the purpose of creating and harvesting stem cells, and Romney refused his support. He said, "Lofty goals do not justify the creation of life for experimentation or destruction."

Romney's views would permit for research the use of embryos about to be destroyed by their parents; this puts him at odds with President Bush's more restrictive position. Romney has never supported state-funded research on embryonic stem cells, and is a believer in the efficacy of alternative methods of producing stem cells.

Source: A Mormon in the White House?, by Hugh Hewitt, p.111-4,
Mar. 12, 2007

Obama on Stem Cells

Stem cells hold promise to cure 70 major diseases

Barack Obama believes we owe it to the American public to explore the potential of stem cells to treat the millions of people suffering from debilitating and life threatening diseases. Stem cells hold the promise of treatments and cures for more than 70 major diseases and conditions such as Parkinson's and Alzheimer's disease, spinal cord injuries, and diabetes. As many as 100 million Americans may benefit from embryonic stem cell research. As president, Obama would:

- Promote Embryonic Stem Cell Research

- Support Medical Advancement and Innovation

- Expand the Number of Stem Cell Lines Available for Research

- Ensure Ethical Standards

Obama introduced legislation in the Illinois Senate to ensure that only those embryos that would otherwise be discarded could be used and that donors would have to provide written consent for the use of the embryos.

Source: Campaign website, BarackObama.com, "Resource Flyers,"
Aug 26, 2007

Notes: Stem Cells are undifferentiated cells, which are useful in disease research. Stem cells are best taken from human fetuses; hence the pro-life opposition. Many pro-life advocates support fetal stem cell research because of the medical potential. In 2001, Pres. Bush announced that the federal policy would be to allow fetal stem cell research on existing stem cell lines but not on new ones.

Romney on Judicial Activism

Firmly pro-life; including Court nominations

Q: [to Santorum]: You are staunchly pro-life. Gov. Romney used to support abortion rights until he changed his position on this a few years ago. Should this be an issue in this primary campaign?

SANTORUM: I think an issue should be looking at the authenticity of that candidate and looking at their record over time and what they fought for. You can look at my record. A lot of folks run for president as pro-life and then that issue gets shoved to the back burner. The issue of pro-life, and the dignity of people at the end of life, those issues will be top priority issues for me to make sure that all life is respected and held with dignity.

ROMNEY: People have had a chance to look at my record and look what I've said. I believe people understand that I'm firmly pro-life. I will support justices who believe in following the Constitution and not legislating from the bench. And I believe in the sanctity of life from the very beginning until the very end.

Source: 2011 GOP primary debate in Manchester NH, June 13, 2011

Obama on Judicial Activism

No litmus test; nominate to Court based on their fairness

Q: Could you ever nominate someone to the Supreme Court who disagrees with you on Roe v. Wade?

McCAIN: I would never, and have never in all the years I've been there, imposed a litmus test on any nominee to the Court. That's not appropriate to do.

OBAMA: Well, I think it's true that we shouldn't apply a strict litmus test and the most important thing in any judge is their capacity to provide fairness and justice to the American people. And it is true that this is going to be, I think, one of the most consequential decisions of the next president. It is very likely that one of us will be making at least one and probably more than one appointments and Roe vs. Wade probably hangs in the balance. I will look for those judges who have an outstanding judicial record, who have the intellect, and who hopefully have a sense of what real-world folks are going through.

Source: Third presidential debate against John McCain, Oct. 15, 2008

Romney on Welfare State

Opportunity is in our DNA; dependency is death to initiative

What is it about American culture that has led us to become the most powerful nation in the history of the world? We believe in hard work and education. We love opportunity: almost all of us are immigrants or descendants of immigrants who came here for opportunity—opportunity is in our DNA. Americans love God, and those who don't have faith, typically believe in something greater than themselves. The values and beliefs of the free American people are the source of our nation's strength and they always will be.

The threat to our culture comes from within. The 1960's welfare programs created a culture of poverty. Some think we won that battle when we reformed welfare, but the liberals haven't given up. At every turn, they try to substitute government largesse for individual responsibility. Dependency is death to initiative, risk-taking and opportunity. Dependency is a culture-killing drug. We have got to fight it like the poison it is.

Source: Speeches to 2008 Conservative Political Action Conference,
Feb. 7, 2008

Obama on Welfare State

Cut poverty in half in 10 years, with faith-based help

Q: In the faith community, we want a new commitment around a measurable goal, something like cutting poverty in half in 10 years. Would you commit to such a goal?

A: I absolutely will make that commitment. I make that commitment with humility because we've got a lot of work to do economically in this country to bring about a more just and fair economy. We've got to shore up the mortgage market. We're going to have to change our tax code. It is a moral imperative to provide health care to every single American. And invest in early childhood education. Many of these can be part of faith-based initiatives I want to keep the Office of Faith-Based Initiatives open, but I want to make sure that its mission is clear. Faith-based initiatives should be targeted specifically at the issue of poverty and how to lift people up.

Source: Democratic Compassion Forum, April 13, 2008

Welfare policies contributed to erosion of black families

A lack of economic opportunity among black men, and the shame and frustration that came from not being able to provide for one's family, contributed to the erosion of black families—a problem that welfare policies for many years may have worsened. And the lack of basic services in so many urban black neighborhoods—parks for kids to play in, police walking the beat, regular garbage pickup, building code enforcement—all helped create a cycle of violence, blight and neglect that continues to haunt us.

Source: Speech on Race, in Change We Can Believe In, p.223-4,
Mar 18, 2008

Romney on Welfare-to-Work

Would require welfare recipients to work

Romney suggested three policy changes: requiring welfare recipients to go to work immediately; eliminating capital gains taxes for firms that invest in inner-city enterprise zones and awarding tax credits for hiring poor residents of those areas; and imposing a crime crackdown with tough mandatory minimum sentences.

Source: Anthony Flint in Boston Globe, Nov. 1, 1994

Vetoed studying how Massachusetts can overcome federal workfare rules

The governor vetoed the part of Budget Item 1599-4408 which authorized a study on potential state responses to federal welfare rule changes. The study would propose methods to maintain existing welfare coverage when federal changes reduced such coverage.

Source: MassScorecard.org item 1599-4408;
roll call 93 passed 130-19, July 14, 2005

Obama on Welfare-to-Work

Welfare recipients know how to succeed but need help

Go into the collar counties around Chicago, and people will tell you they don't want their tax money wasted by a welfare agency or the Pentagon. Go into any inner city neighborhood, and folks will tell you that government alone can't teach our kids to learn. They know that parents have to parent, that children can't achieve unless we raise their expectations and turn off the television sets and eradicate the slander that says a black youth with a book is acting white. They know those things.

Source: Keynote speech to the Democratic National Convention,
Jul 29, 2004

Belief that "I am my brother's keeper" makes America work

Obama emphasized a sense of shared values in the 2004 Democratic Convention speech: "Alongside our famous individualism, there's another ingredient in the American saga. A believe that we are connected as one people. If there's a child on the south side of Chicago who can't read, that matters to me, even if it's not my child. If there's a senior citizen somewhere who can't pay for her prescription and has to choose between medicine and the rent, that makes my life poorer, even if it's not my grandmother. It's that fundamental belief—I am my brother's keeper. I am my sister's keeper—that makes this country work."

Source: The 100 Greatest Speeches, by Kourdi & Maier, p.197,
Jul 1, 2004

Romney on Don't-Ask-Don't-Tell

Don't ask, don't tell: sounds silly, but it's effective

Q: In 1994 you were quoted as saying that you advocated gays being able to serve openly and honestly in our nation's military. Do you still feel that way?

ROMNEY: No, actually, when I first heard of the "Don't ask, don't tell" policy, I thought it sounded awfully silly. I didn't think that would be very effective. And I turned out to be wrong. It's been the policy now in the military for what, 10, 15 years, and it seems to be working. This is not the time to put in place a major change, a social experiment, in the middle of a war going on. I wouldn't change it at this point. We can look at down the road. But it does seem to me that we have much bigger issues as a nation we ought to be talking about than that policy right now.

McCAIN: I think it would be a terrific mistake to even reopen the issue. The policy is working. And I am convinced that that's the way we can maintain this greatest military. Let's not tamper with them.

Source: GOP debate at Saint Anselm College, June 3, 2007

Obama on Don't-Ask-Don't-Tell

Repeal Don't-Ask-Don't-Tell

Obama believes we need to repeal the "don't ask, don't tell" policy in consultation with military commanders. The key test for military service should be patriotism, a sense of duty, and a willingness to serve. Obama will work with military leaders to repeal the current policy and ensure we accomplish our national defense goals.

Source: Campaign website, BarackObama.com, "Resource Flyers,"
Aug 26, 2007

NOTE: The policy banning open homosexuals serving in the military was repealed on Sept. 20, 2011. Hence gay and lesbian people may now openly serve in the US military. Since 1993, the DADT policy held that homosexuals may serve as long as they do not announce their homosexuality ("Don't Tell"), but also that the military may not investigate their homosexuality ("Don't Ask").

Romney on Defense of Marriage Act

MA Constitution, by John Adams, has no same-sex marriage

I've been in a state that has gay marriage, and I recognize that the consequences of gay marriage fall far beyond just the relationship between a man and a woman. They also relate to our kids and the right of religion to be practiced freely in a society.

The status of marriage, if it's allowed among the same sex individuals in one state is going to spread to the entire nation. And that's why it's important to have a national standard for marriage. And I'm committed to making sure that we reinforce the institution of marriage in this country by insisting that all states have a right to have marriage as defined as between a man and a woman; and we don't have unelected judges saying we're going to impose same-sex marriage where it was clearly not in their state constitution.

My state's constitution was written by John Adams. It isn't there. I've looked. The people need to speak on this issue and make sure that marriage is preserved as between a man and a woman.

Source: 2007 GOP primary debate in Orlando, Florida, Oct. 21, 2007

NOTE: "DOMA" refers to the Defense of Marriage Act, passed by Congress in 1996, which defined marriage as consisting of one man and one woman (in other words, barring same-sex marriage). DOMA applies to all federal benefits and taxes, but not necessarily to state benefits and taxes.

Obama on Defense of Marriage Act

Decisions about marriage should be left to the states

One of Obama's pragmatic stands troubling to progressives is on gay marriage. In the Senate debate, Obama opposed the right-wing Federal Marriage Amendment to ban gay marriage nationally and said: "I agree with most Americans, with Democrats and Republicans, with Vice President Cheney, with over 2,000 religious leaders of all different beliefs, that decisions about marriage, as they always have, should be left to the states." However, Obama also declared, "Personally, I do believe that marriage is between a man and a woman." At the same time, Obama has strongly supported civil unions, arguing that it is a way to protect equal rights without taking the politically risky approach of gay marriage.

Source: The Improbable Quest, by John K. Wilson, p.114-5,
Oct 30, 2007

Marriage not a human right; non-discrimination is

Q: Do you think marriage is a human right?

A: I don't think marriage is a civil right, but I think that not being discriminated against is a civil right. I think making sure that we don't engage in the sort of gay-bashing that, I think, has unfortunately dominated this campaign-not just here in Illinois, but across the country-is unfortunate, and that kind of mean-spirited attacks on homosexuals is something that the people of Illinois generally have rejected.

Source: IL Senate Debate, Oct. 26, 2004

Romney on Affirmative Action

Failure to educate minorities is a civil rights issue

The "achievement gap" has been lamented for decades but distressingly little has been done to combat it. About half of African American and Hispanic American students drop out before receiving a high-school degree. The result is that we are virtually assuring the creation of permanent underclass. It is an inexplicable human tragedy when millions of American children barely attain a third-world education in a nation that offers all its citizens access to free public schooling. Our current failure to educate our minority populations is the foremost civil-rights issue of our generation.

The minority proportion of the US population is projected to rise from 26% today to 34% by 2030, and if the achievement gap and dropout rate among minorities continues, the average educational level of the nation's entire workforce will continue to decline dramatically.

Source: No Apology, by Mitt Romney, p.198-199, March 2, 2010

To compete as a nation, draw on skills of women & minorities

Women that I have seen in organizations have not had the opportunity that they deserve to have in getting ahead in organizations. If we are to compete as a nation, we've got to draw on the skills of women and minorities. And I have seen organizations from the federal government to corporations that are not drawing on the skills of women and minorities.

Source: MA Senate Debate with Ted Kennedy, Oct. 1, 1994

Obama on Affirmative Action

Include class-based affirmative action with race-based

Obama declared his daughters "should probably be treated by any admissions officer as folks who are pretty advantaged. I think that we should take into account white kids who have been disadvantaged and have grown up in poverty and shown themselves to have what it takes to succeed."

But Obama is not race blind, and neither is his ideal of affirmative action, which would combine both race-based and class-based preferences. He said, "I don't think those concepts are mutually exclusive. I think what one can say is that in our society race and class still intersect, and there are a lot of African American kids who are struggling, that even those who are in the middle class may be first generation as opposed to fifth or sixth generation college attendees, and that we all have an interest in bringing as many people together to help build this country."

Source: The Improbable Quest, by John K. Wilson, p. 65-6, Oct. 30, 2007

Racial equality good for America as a whole

Q: Is race still the most intractable issue in America?

A: We have made enormous progress, but the progress we have made is not good enough. We live in a society that remains separated in terms of life opportunities for African-Americans, for Latinos, and the rest of the nation. But there has also got to be a social responsibility, there has to be a sense of mutual responsibility, and there's got to be political will in the White House to make that happen.

Source: Democratic Primary Debate at Howard University, June 28, 2007

Romney on College Loans

China and India graduate
more science and engineering PhDs

Increasing productivity begins with innovation and innovation begins with good ideas. More often than not, good ideas come from educated minds. America's post-WWII commitment to public higher education directly contributed to the burst of productivity that rocketed our economy beyond every other. But other nations have made as great or greater a commitment to higher education than we have, particularly in engineering, computer science, and information. 15 years ago, China and India awarded about half as many master's degrees in these fields as did the US. Today, they graduate more than two times the number of students in these fields as we do.

While our annual number of degrees has hovered around 7,000 to 8,000, China's has risen from 1,784 to 12,130—50% greater than ours. This is a stunning reversal of global preeminence in the priority attached to the highest level of educational attainment. Not surprisingly, China, Japan, and Taiwan claim a growing share of the world's patents.

Source: No Apology, by Mitt Romney, p.120, March 2, 2010

Obama on College Loans

$10K college tax credit; forgive loans for public service

In this economy, a high school diploma no longer guarantees a good job. That's why I urge the Senate to pass a bill that will revitalize our community colleges, which are a career pathway to the children of so many working families.

To make college more affordable, this bill will finally end the unwarranted taxpayer subsidies that go to banks for student loans. Instead, let's take that money and give families a $10,000 tax credit for four years of college & increase Pell Grants.

And let's tell another one million students that when they graduate, they will be required to pay only 10% of their income on student loans, and all of their debt will be forgiven after 20 years—and forgiven after 10 years if they choose a career in public service, because in the USA, no one should go broke because they chose to go to college.

And by the way, it's time for colleges and universities to get serious about cutting their own costs—because they, too, have a responsibility to help solve this problem.

Source: State of the Union Address, Jan. 27, 2010

Romney on No Child Left Behind

Changed from closing Education Dept. to supporting NCLB

Q: You have been criticized for changing your position on some issues. You say that it's a part of learning from experience. Can you point to an area in which your learning from experience led you to change to a position that is less popular with the Republican base?

A: Sure, quite a few, actually. One is No Child Left Behind. I've taken a position where, once upon a time, I said I wanted to eliminate the Department of Education. That was my position when I ran for Senate in 1994. That's very popular with the base. As I've been a governor and seen the impact that the federal government can have holding down the interest of the teachers' unions and instead putting the interests of the kids and the parents and the teachers first, I see that the Department of Education can actually make a difference. So I supported No Child Left Behind. I still do. I know there are a lot in my party that don't like it, but I like testing in our schools. I think it allows us to get better schools.

Source: 2007 Republican Debate in South Carolina, May 15, 2007

Obama on No Child Left Behind

We need real commitment to education; instead we got NCLB

These past eight years will be remembered for misguided policies & missed opportunities. We still have no real strategy to compete in a global economy. Just think of what we could have done. We could have made a real commitment to a world-class education for our kids, but instead we passed "No Child Left Behind," a law that—however well-intended—left the money behind and alienated teachers and principals instead of inspiring them.

I want to take us in a new and better direction. It's time for new policies that create the jobs & opportunities of the future—a competitiveness agenda built upon education and energy, innovation and infrastructure, fair trade and reform.

This agenda starts with education. A highly-educated and skilled workforce will be the key not only to individual opportunity, but to the overall success of our economy as well. We cannot be satisfied until every child in America—and I mean every child—has the same chances for a good education that we want for our own children.

Source: Speech in Flint, MI, in Change We Can Believe In, pp.246-7,
Jun 15, 2008

Romney on School Vouchers

Supported means-tested vouchers
for public & private schools

- Pledged to vote to establish a means-tested school voucher program to allow students to attend the public or private school of their choice.

- Supported abolishing the federal Department of Education

- Favored keeping control of educational reform at the lowest level, closest to parents, teachers, and the community.

Source: Boston Globe review of 1994 campaign issues, Mar. 21, 2002

School choice over fat-cat CEOs of teachers' unions

Our conservative agenda strengthens our family in part by, by putting our schools on track to be the best in the world again, because great schools start with great teachers. We'll insist on hiring teachers from the top third college graduates and we'll give better teachers better pay. School accountability, school choice, cyber schools will be priorities and we'll put parents and teachers back in charge of education, not fat-cat CEOs of the teachers' unions.

Source: Speech to 2010 Conservative Political Action Conference,
Feb. 20, 2010

Obama on School Vouchers

Vouchers don't solve the problems of our schools

McCAIN: I'm sure you're aware, Sen. Obama, of the program in the Washington, D.C., school system where vouchers are provided. It's a thousand and some 9,000 parents asked to be eligible for that.

OBAMA: The D.C. school system is in terrible shape, and it has been for a very long time. And we've got a wonderful new superintendent there who's working very hard with the young mayor.

McCAIN: Who supports vouchers.

OBAMA: Actually, she supports charters.

McCAIN: She supports vouchers, also.

OBAMA: Even if Sen. McCain were to say that vouchers were the way to go—I disagree with him on this, because the data doesn't show that it actually solves the problem—the centerpiece of Sen. McCain's education policy is to increase the voucher program in D.C. by 2,000 slots. That leaves all of you who live in the other 50 states without an education reform policy from Sen. McCain.

McCAIN: Because there's not enough vouchers; therefore, we shouldn't do it, even though it's working. I got it.

Source: Third presidential debate against John McCain, Oct. 15, 2008

Romney on Fathers In Families

Child development enhanced
by having a mother & father

The attack on faith & religion is no less relentless. Tolerance for pornography and sexual promiscuity, combined with the twisted incentives of government welfare programs have led to today's grim realities: 68% of African American children are born out-of-wedlock; 45% of Hispanic children; 25% of White children. How much harder it is for these children to succeed in school and in life. A nation built on the principles of the Founding Fathers cannot long stand when its children are raised without fathers in the home.

The development of a child is enhanced by having a mother and father. Such a family is the ideal for the future of the child and for the strength of a nation. I wonder how it is that unelected judges, like some in my state of Massachusetts, are so unaware of this reality, so oblivious to the millennia of recorded history. It is time for the people of America to fortify marriage through Constitutional amendment, so that liberal judges cannot continue to attack it.

Source: Speeches to 2008 Conservative Political Action Conference,
Feb. 7, 2008

Obama on Fathers In Families

I know what it means to have an absent father

I know what it means to have an absent father, although my circumstances weren't as tough as they are for many young people today. Even though my father left us when I was two years old, I was luckier than most. I screwed up more often than I should've, but I got plenty of second chances. A lot of kids don't get these chances today. There is no margin for error in their lives.

Still, I know the toll that being a single parent took on my mother—how she struggled at times to the pay bills; to give us the things that other kids had; to play all the roles that both parents are supposed to play. And I know the toll it took on me. So I resolved many years ago that it was my obligation to break the cycle—that if I could be anything in life, I would be a good father to my girls; that if I could give them anything, I would give them that rock—that foundation—on which to build their lives. And that would be the greatest gift I could offer.

Source: Chicago church speech, in Change We Can Believe In, p.236,
Jun 15, 2008

Romney on the Tea Party

Me & Tea Party are both
for small government & low spending

Q: Are you a member of the Tea Party?

ROMNEY: I don't think you carry cards in the Tea Party. I believe in a lot of what the Tea Party believes in. The Tea Party believes that government's too big, and taxing too much. I put together a plan with a whole series of points of how we can get America's economy going again. Tea Party people like that. So if the Tea Party is for keeping government small and spending down, and helping us create jobs, then, hey, I'm for the Tea Party.

Source: GOP debate in Simi Valley CA at the Reagan Library, Sept. 7, 2011

Obama on the Tea Party

92% of Tea Partiers:
"Obama is moving US toward socialism"

By April 2010, over half of the nation—and 92 percent of Tea Partiers—believed that President Obama was moving the country toward socialism. Combine our anxiety over the meltdown with today's downward economic mobility, and you get scapegoating run amok. A Harris Poll in March 2010 showed that, among Republicans, 57 percent believe Obama is a Muslim, 38 percent believe he "is doing many of the things that Hitler did," and 24 percent believe that the president "may be the Anti-Christ."

Source: Third World America, by Arianna Huffington, p. 86, Sept. 2, 2010

NOTE: "Socialism" is represented by a legal political party in the United States, and in numerous countries abroad. The Socialist Party of America runs candidates for president (Brian Moore in 2008, for example), and has numerous elected mayors around the country. One member of the Senate, Bernie Sanders from Vermont, calls himself a socialist, but is not a member of the Socialist Party.

When Pres. Obama is accused of "moving the country toward socialism," his accusers do not imply that he is secretly a member of the Socialist Party, but do imply that he ascribes to that party's beliefs. Those beliefs focus on high progressive taxation; redistribution of wealth; and providing a wide array of social services free of charge. Most importantly, Socialists propose achieving those goals by revolutionary transformation as opposed to gradual changes, and reject policies like ObamaCare as too gradual. Obama's policies are indeed closer to the Socialist Party's positions than are the Republican Party's—but Obama has never advocated revolutionary transformation!

Romney on Personal Faith

My faith would inform my presidency

Kennedy's famous speech [on Catholicism in 1960] is actually quite different from the way it is often described. Instead of reconciling his religious identity with his role in public life, Kennedy entirely separated the two.

In the 2008 Republican primary, Massachusetts governor Mitt Romney's Mormon faith was likewise perceived as an issue by some voters. Claiming that many would be reluctant to pull the lever for a person of his beliefs, some pundits and political advisors urged him to "do a JFK." Just give a speech, they told him, and reassure voters that your faith will have nothing to do with your presidency. Instead, he gave a thoughtful speech that eloquently and correctly described the role of faith in American public life.

Unlike JFK, Romney declared that our religious liberty is "fundamental to America's greatness." And he spoke openly of "how my faith would inform my presidency, if elected."

Source: America by Heart, by Sarah Palin, p.184-5, Nov. 23, 2010

Obama on Personal Faith

I am a person of faith; and I reach out to people of faith

CLINTON: [about Obama's comment that people in small towns get bitter and they cling to guns & religion]: I think that is a fundamental misunderstanding of the role of faith in times that are good and times that are bad.

OBAMA: Hillary has been saying I'm elitist, out of touch, condescending. Let me be absolutely clear. It would be pretty hard for me to be condescending towards people of faith, since I'm a person of faith and have done more than most other campaigns in reaching out specifically to people of faith, and have written about how Democrats make an error when they don't show up and speak directly to people's faith. The same is true with respect to gun owners. I have large numbers of sportsmen and gun owners in my home state, and they have supported me precisely because I have listened to them.

Source: Philadelphia primary debate, on eve of PA primary, April 16, 2008

First American president not raised in a Christian home

If Obama ascends to the presidency, he will be the first American president to do so having not been raised in a Christian home. Instead, he spent his early years under the influence of atheism, folk Islam, and a humanist's understanding of the world that sees religion merely as a man-made thing, as a product of psychology. It is this departure from tradition in Obama's early years that makes both his political journey and his religious journey so unusual and of such symbolic meaning.

Source: The Faith of Barack Obama, by Stephen Mansfield, Aug. 5, 2008

Romney on Religious Values

Americans want person of faith as president, whatever brand

One by one the other presidential campaigns have committed "accidental" attacks on Romney's religion. The presidential candidates were all quick to apologize for the actions of their campaign workers. In each case the candidates expressed regret and disappointment as they disavowed any attacks on religion. All stressed that they disavowed any attacks on religion. All stressed that they wanted to run a clean campaign that would not tolerate bigotry.

Gov. Romney accepted the apologies, saying, "Clearly, any derogatory comments about anyone's faith—those comments are troubling. The fact they keep on coming up is even more troubling."

It's not all negative, however. At an early campaign stop a man in the audience challenged Romney directly, telling him that he would surely go to hell. The crowd groaned, then booed the man. Romney responded with what has become his signature comment on religion. "I believe Americans want a person of faith to lead the country. It doesn't matter what brand."

Source: The Man, His Values, & His Vision, p. 93-95, Aug. 31, 2007

Obama on Religious Values

Listening to evangelicals bridges major political fault line

Today, white evangelical Christians are the heart and soul of the Republican Party's grassroots base. It is their issues—abortion, gay marriage, prayer in schools, intelligent design, Terri Schiavo, the posting of the Ten Commandments in the courthouse, home schooling, voucher plans, and the makeup of the Supreme Court— that often dominate the headlines and serve as one of the major fault lines in American politics. The single biggest gap in party affiliation is between those who attend church regularly and those who don't. Democrats, meanwhile, are scrambling to "get religion," even as a core segment of our constituency remains stubbornly secular, and fears that the agenda of an assertively Christian nation may not make room for them or their life choices.

The evangelists' success points to a hunger for the product they are selling, a hunger that goes beyond any particular issue or cause. They need an assurance that somebody out there cares about them, is listening to them.

Source: The Audacity of Hope, by Barack Obama, p.201–2, Oct. 1, 2006

Romney vs. Obama on International Issues

International issues focus on foreign relations and anything involving foreign nations, including the following topics:

- *Energy and Oil:* including global warming, domestic drilling and alternative energy sources. Romney wants domestic oil drilling and both candidates suggest nuclear power. Romney accepts global warming but wants international participation while Obama would start in the US.

- *Free Trade:* including NAFTA (the North American Free trade Agreement) and other bilateral agreements, plus opinions on the trade organizations like the WTO (World Trade Organization). Romney wants to push China; Obama is more cautious.

- *Immigration:* including border security; the border fence; and dealing with the current 12 million illegal immigrants in the US. Romney focuses on reducing immigrant benefits; Obama focuses on avoiding anti-immigrant attitudes.

- *Foreign Policy:* Romney focuses on military solutions in Iran and elsewhere, justified as "spreading democracy." Obama believes in the United Nations and believes in talking with other countries, even our enemies.

- *Homeland Security:* This category includes defense spending issues and defense strategy goals. Romney wants dramatic increases in defense spending and no change in terrorism policy; Obama wants small increases in defense spending and incremental changes in terrorism policy.

- *War and Peace:* including the current ongoing wars in Iraq and Afghanistan. Obama has officially ended the Iraq War but maintains troops in Afghanistan, Kuwait, and elsewhere. Romney disagrees with withdrawing from either country.

Mitt Romney on International Issues

Barack Obama
on International Issues

Romney on Climate Change

They don't call it "America warming" but "global warming"

When you put in place a new cap or a mandate, and particularly if you don't have any safety valve as to how much the cost of that cap might be, you would impose on the American people, if you do it unilaterally, without involving all the world, you'd impose on the American people a huge new effective tax: 20% on utilities, 50 cents a gallon for gasoline—that's according to the energy information agency—would be imposed on us. What happens if you do that? You put a big burden on energy in this country as the energy-intensive industries say, "We're going to move our new facilities from the US to China, where they don't have those agreements." You end up polluting and putting just as much CO_2 in the air because the big energy users go there. That's why these ideas make sense, but only on a global basis. They don't call it "America warming." They call it "global warming." That's why you've got to have a president that understands the real economy.

Source: 2008 Republican debate at Reagan Library in Simi Valley,
Jan. 30, 2008

NOTE: "Cap-and-Trade" refers to a carbon dioxide (CO_2) emissions policy where the amount of CO_2 is "capped" at a government-specified emission amount, and then the right to emit CO_2 is "traded" via emission permits. A similar program was used successfully to battle acid rain via sulfur dioxide emission permits trading on the Chicago Mercantile Exchange.

Obama on Climate Change

Aggressively address accelerating climate change

Q: What do you think the toughest choice you have left to make is?

A: The issue of climate change. I've put forward one of the most aggressive proposals out there, but the science seems to be coming in indicating it's accelerating even more quickly with every passing day. And by the time I take office, I think we're going to have to have a serious conversation about how drastic steps we need to take to address it.

Source: Democratic radio debate on NPR, Dec. 4, 2007

Cap-and-trade carbon emissions; raise CAFE standard

It's time to turn the page on energy, to break the stalemate that's kept our fuel efficiency standards in the same place for 20 years, to tell the oil and auto industries that they must act, not only because their future's at stake, but because the future of our country and our planet is at stake.

As president, I will place a cap on carbon emissions and require companies who can't meet the cap to buy credits from those who can, which will generate billions of dollars to invest in renewable sources of energy and create new jobs and even a new industry in the process. I'll put in place a low carbon fuel standard that will take 50 million cars worth of pollution off the road. I'll raise the fuel efficiency standards for our cars and trucks because we know we have the technology to do it and it's the time to do it.

Source: Take Back America 2007 Conference, June 19, 2007

Romney on Oil Drilling

Develop alternative energy but also drill in ANWR

To remain the economic and military superpower, America must address achieving energy independence. We must become independent from foreign sources of oil. This will mean a combination of efforts related to conservation and efficiency measures, developing alternative sources of energy like biodiesel, ethanol, nuclear, and coal gasification, and finding more domestic sources of oil such as in ANWR or the Outer Continental Shelf (OCS).

Source: PAC website, www.TheCommonwealthPac.com, "Meet Mitt,"
Dec 1, 2006

NOTES: "ANWR" refers to the Arctic National Wildlife Refuge, a protected area in northern Alaska that contains substantial supplies of oil and gas. Conservatives favor drilling ANWR to extract the oil, while liberals favor maintaining its protected status.

"OCS" refers to drilling for oil off the Outer Continental Shelf, several miles offshore. States control oil drilling in waters up to three miles offshore; the federal government controls waters from that distance until the continental shelf ends and the deep ocean begins (a maximum of about 350 miles offshore). Conservatives favor OCS drilling to reach more potential oil reserves; liberals cite the greater technical challenges and the higher risk of oil spills.

Obama on Oil Drilling

We cannot drill our way out of our addiction to oil

It is hard to overstate the degree to which our addiction to oil undermines our future. Without any change to energy policy, US demand for oil will jump 40% in 20 years. Over the same period, worldwide demand will jump 30%.

A large portion of the $800 million we spend on foreign oil every day goes to some of the world's most volatile regimes. And there are the environmental consequences. Just about every scientist outside the White House believes climate change is real.

We cannot drill our way out of the problem. Instead of subsidizing the oil industry, we should end every single tax break the industry currently receives and demand that 1% of the revenues from oil companies with over $1 billion in quarterly profits go toward financing alternative energy research and infrastructure.

Over the last 30 years, countries like Brazil have used a mix of regulation and direct government investment to develop a biofuel industry; 70% of its new vehicles run on sugar-based ethanol.

Source: The Audacity of Hope, by Barack Obama, p.167-9, Oct. 1, 2006

Romney on Nuclear Power

Develop energy technology like nuclear or liquefied coal

We face serious competitive challenges globally unless we become serious with getting prices of energy down. It's a great opportunity for America to develop technology to lead the world in energy efficiency as well as energy production. And whether it's nuclear or liquefied coal, where we sequester the CO_2, far more fuel-efficient automobiles. These are some of the incentives that have to be behind our policies with regards to our investments in new technologies like ethanol.

Source: 2007 Republican debate in Dearborn, Michigan, Oct. 9, 2007

NOTES: "Carbon sequestration" refers to removing CO_2 (carbon dioxide) from the atmosphere and keeping it "sequestered," or captured and stored, in a way that the CO_2 cannot return to the atmosphere. Nature performs the simplest form of carbon sequestration: growing trees, which convert CO_2 into wood. Human methods include chemical processes; burying CO_2 underground; or mineralization (converting to carbonate rocks).

"Clean coal" refers to implementing methods for carbon capture and storage at coal-burning plants. Sequestering CO_2 from coal plants involves filtering smokestack emissions (called "CO_2 scrubbing"); capturing CO_2 gas; and chemical conversion into stable solids. As of 2012, some smokestack experiments successfully demonstrate the techniques, but none are yet in commercial use.

Obama on Nuclear Power

Nuclear power ok if we safeguard against waste & terrorism

Q: Would you be in favor of developing more nuclear power to reduce oil dependency?

A: I don't think that we can take nuclear power off the table. What we have to make sure of is that we have the capacity to store waste properly and safely, and that we reduce whatever threats might come from terrorism. And if we can do that in a technologically sound way, then we should pursue it. If we can't, we should not. But there is no magic bullet on energy. We're going to have to look at all the various options.

Source: Democratic primary debate at Dartmouth College, Sept. 6, 2007

More incentives for clean energy, including nuclear

To create more clean energy jobs, we need more production, more efficiency, more incentives. And that means building a new generation of safe, clean nuclear power plants in this country. It means making tough decisions about opening new offshore areas for oil and gas development. It means continued investment in advanced biofuels and clean coal technologies. And, yes, it means passing a comprehensive energy and climate bill with incentives that will finally make clean energy profitable.

Source: State of the Union Address, Jan. 27, 2010

Romney on China Trade

China doesn't want to have a trade war; so push hard

Q: Candidates have talked tough on China before—George W. Bush did it, Barack Obama did it—but once elected, the president takes a much more cautious approach.

A: They have been played like a fiddle by the Chinese. And the Chinese are smiling all the way to the bank, taking our currency and taking our jobs and taking a lot of our future. And I'm not willing to let that happen. We've got to call cheating for what it is.

Q: Isn't that risking a trade war?

A: Well, now, think about that. We buy this much stuff from China; they buy that much stuff from us. You think they want to have a trade war? This is a time when we're being hollowed out by China that is artificially holding down their prices. On day one, I will issue an executive order identifying China as a currency manipulator. We'll bring an action against them in front of the WTO for manipulating their currency. If you're not willing to stand up to China, you'll get run over by China. And that's what's happened for 20 years.

Source: GOP debate at Dartmouth College, NH, Oct. 11, 2011

NOTE: "WTO" refers to the World Trade Organization, an international organization intended to reduce trade barriers, formed in 1995. WTO members (which include China since 2001) charge minimal import tariffs on each other. The WTO adjudicates international disputes over trade barriers, such as currency manipulation.

Obama on China Trade

China is a competitor but not an enemy

Q: Given China's size, its muscular manufacturing capabilities, its military buildup, at this point—and also including its large trade deficit—at this point, who has more leverage, China or the U.S.?

A: Number one is we've got to get our own fiscal house in order. Number two, when I was visiting Africa, I was told by a group of businessmen that the presence of China is only exceeded by the absence of America in the entire African continent. Number three, we have to be tougher negotiators with China. They are not enemies, but they are competitors of ours. Right now the United States is still the dominant superpower in the world. But the next president can't be thinking about today; he or she also has to be thinking about 10 years from now, 20 years from now, 50 years from now.

Source: Des Moines Register Democratic debate, Dec. 13, 2007

U.S. needs to ameliorate trade relations with China

The U.S. should be firm on issues that divide us like Taiwan while flexible on issues that could unite us. We should insist on labor standards and human rights, the opening of Chinese markets fully to American goods, and the fulfillment of legal contracts with American businesses but without triggering a trade war as prolonged instability in the Chinese economy could have global economic consequences.

Source: In His Own Words, edited by Lisa Rogak, p. 22, March 27, 2007

Romney on Immigrant Benefits

Turn off the magnet that attracts immigrants

I learned this when I was with border patrol agents in San Diego, and they said, look, they can always get a ladder to go over the fence. And people will always run to the country. The reason they come in such great numbers is because we've left the magnet on.

And I said, what do you mean, the magnet? And they said, when employers are willing to hire people who are here illegally, that's a magnet, and it draws them in. And sanctuary cities, giving tuition breaks to the kids of illegal aliens, employers that knowingly hire people who are here illegally. Those things also have to be stopped.

If we want to secure the border, we have to make sure we have a fence, determining where people are, enough agents to oversee it, & turn off that magnet. We can't talk about amnesty, we cannot give amnesty to those who have come here illegally.

We've got 4.7 million people waiting in line legally. Let those people come in first, and those that are here illegally, they shouldn't have a special deal.

Source: 2011 GOP debate in Simi Valley CA at the Reagan Library,
Sept. 7, 2011

Obama on Immigrant Benefits

Pathway to citizenship, but people have to earn it

Q: Are you going to create a path to the citizenship for undocumented workers?

A: We have to make sure that employers are held accountable, because right now employers are taking advantage of undocumented workers. And we've got to give a pathway to citizenship. But people have to earn it. They're going to have to pay a fine. They've got to make sure that they're learning English. They've got to go to the back of the line so that they're not rewarded for having broken the law.

Source: AFL-CIO Democratic primary forum, Aug. 8, 2007

Provide funding for social services for noncitizens

Obama co-sponsored an amendment providing funding for social services for noncitizens:

OFFICIAL CONGRESSIONAL SUMMARY: To establish a grant program to provide financial assistance to States and local governments for the costs of providing health care and educational services to noncitizens, and to provide additional funding for the State Criminal Alien Assistance Program (SCAAP).

SPONSOR'S INTRODUCTORY REMARKS: Sen. CLINTON: our failed national immigration policy has left our State and local governments to bear the brunt of the cost of immigration. My amendment provides financial assistance for the cost of health and educational services related to immigration.

Source: SCAAP Funding (S.AMDT.4072 to S.2611) on May 18, 2006

Romney on Guest Workers

I like legal immigration; let business determine visas

Q: In 2008, you said you favored allowing American companies to hire more skilled foreign workers. With unemployment at 9.1%, are you still for importing more foreign labor?

A: Well, of course not. We're not looking to bring people in for jobs that can be done by Americans. But at the same time, we want to make sure that America welcomes the best and brightest in the world. If someone comes here and gets a PhD in physics, that's the person I'd like to staple a green card to their diploma, rather than saying to them to go home. I want the best & brightest to be metered into the country based upon the needs of our employment sector & create jobs by bringing technology and innovation that comes from people around the world. I like legal immigration I'd have the number of visas that we give to people here that come here legally, determined in part by the needs of our employment community. But we have to secure our border and crack down on those that bring folks here and hire here illegally.

Source: Iowa Straw Poll GOP debate in Ames Iowa, Aug. 11, 2011

Obama on Guest Workers

Anti-immigrant bitterness stems from joblessness

Obama said at a private fund-raiser in San Francisco, "You go into some of the small towns in Pennsylvania, and like a lot of small towns in the Midwest, the jobs have been gone now for 25 years and nothing's replaced them. So it's not surprising then that [people there] get bitter, they cling to guns or religion or antipathy to people who aren't like them or anti-immigrant sentiment or anti-trade sentiment as a way to explain their frustrations."

Obama's "bitter/cling" comments seemed to [indicate] that he was, at bottom, a helpless and hopeless elitist.

Source: Game Change, by Heilemann & Halpern, p.240-1,
Jan 11, 2010

Crack down on employers who hire illegal immigrants

Obama wants to remove incentives for illegals to enter the country by cracking down on employers who hire undocumented immigrants. Obama has championed a proposal to create a system so employers can verify that their employees are legally eligible to work in the US. Obama recognizes that immigration raids are ineffective, netting only 3,600 arrests in 2006.

Obama's priority is to stop the current illegal immigration into the United States, and then deal compassionately and fairly with the illegal immigrants who re already living here. If the flood of new immigrants can be slowed considerably, Obama believes that those currently living here, over time, can be effectively absorbed into the population and the economy.

Source: Obamanomics, by John R. Talbott, p.120-1, July 1, 2008

Romney on American Exceptionalism

American Exceptionalism means
America need not decline

In a world composed of nations that are filled with rage and hate for the US, our president should proudly defend her rather than continually apologize for her. I reject the view that America must decline. I believe in American exceptionalism. I am convinced that we can act together to strengthen the nation, to preserve our global leadership, and to protect freedom where it exits and promote it where it does not. What is ahead of us now will not be easy.

It will be difficult to overcome the challenges we face, to maintain our national strength and purpose even as China, Russia, and the jihadists pursue their own ambitions. It will be difficult to repair the damage from the economic panic of 2008 and the intemperate actions that have been justified as steps to remedy it. I don't worry about our ability to overcome any problem or threat. But I do wonder whether we will take this action that is timely, and that we will act before the necessary correction is massively disruptive.

Source: No Apology, by Mitt Romney, pp. 29&33, March 2, 2010

NOTE: "American exceptionalism" means that America has a unique status in the world today. The interest in American exceptionalism counters Obama's rejection of the concept, when Obama said, "Sure, I believe in American exceptionalism in the same way the British believe in British exceptionalism." Republicans generally interpret that as meaning, "No, I don't believe in your version of American exceptionalism at all."

Obama on American Exceptionalism

American exceptionalism is same as any other exceptionalism

Many people don't believe we have special message for the world or a special mission to preserve our greatness for the betterment of not just ourselves but all of humanity. Astonishingly, President Obama even said that he believes in American exceptionalism in the same way "the Brits believe in British exceptionalism and the Greeks believe in Greek exceptionalism." Which is to say, he doesn't believe in American exceptionalism at all. He seems to think it is just a kind of irrational prejudice in favor of our way of life. To me, that is appalling.

When President Obama insists that all countries are exceptional, he's saying that none is, last of all the country he leads. That's a shame, because American exceptionalism is something that people in both parties used to believe in.

Source: America by Heart, by Sarah Palin, p. 69, Nov. 23, 2010

Romney on Iranian Sanctions

Unacceptable for Iran to become a nuclear nation

Q: How would you approach the new reality for our ally, Israel, and the existential threats it faces from Iran, Hamas, and Hezbollah?

ROMNEY: Very simple. You start off by saying that you don't allow an inch of space to exist between you and your friends and your allies. The president went about this all wrong. He went around the world and apologized for America. He addressed the United Nations in his inaugural address and chastised our friend, Israel, for building settlements and said nothing about Hamas launching thousands of rockets into Israel.

The right course for us is to stand behind our friends, to listen to them, and to let the entire world know that we will stay with them and that we will support them and defend them. And with regards to Iran, which perhaps represents the greatest existential threat to Israel, we have to make it abundantly clear: It is unacceptable—and I take that word carefully—it is unacceptable for Iran to become a nuclear nation.

Source: GOP Google debate in Orlando FL, Sept. 22, 2011

Obama on Iranian Sanctions

Iran is more isolated and will face growing consequences

Diplomatic efforts have strengthened our hand in dealing with those nations that insist on violating international agreements in pursuit of nuclear weapons. That's why North Korea now faces increased isolation, and stronger sanctions—sanctions that are being vigorously enforced. That's why the international community is more united, and the Islamic Republic of Iran is more isolated. And as Iran's leaders continue to ignore their obligations: They, too, will face growing consequences.

Source: State of the Union Address, Jan. 27, 2010

Must be tough on Iran, but talk to them too

Q: How big a threat is Iran to the US?

A: What we've seen over the last several years is Iran's influence grow. So our policy over the last eight years has not worked. We cannot tolerate a nuclear Iran. Not only would it threaten Israel, a country that is our stalwart ally, but it would also set off an arms race in the Middle East.

We are going to have to engage in tough direct diplomacy with Iran and this is a major difference I have with Senator McCain, this notion by not talking to people we are punishing them has not worked. It has not worked in Iran, it has not worked in North Korea. In each instance, our efforts of isolation have actually accelerated their efforts to get nuclear weapons.

Source: First presidential debate, Obama vs. McCain, Sept. 26, 2008

Romney on International Diplomacy

Encourage others to welcome democracy, without military

Q: President Bush said in his second inaugural address, "It is the policy of the US to seek and support the growth of democratic movements and institutions in every nation and culture." Has President Bush's policy been a success, with all the elections going on?

A: Democracy is not defined by a vote. There have to be the underpinnings of democracy: education, health care, people recognizing they live in a place that has the rule of law. And that's why our effort to spread democracy should continue, not to just spread votes, but instead to encourage other people in the world to have the benefits that we enjoy and to welcome democracy. There's no question in this country, we need to reach out, not just with our military might—although that we have, and should keep it strong—but also reach out with our other great capabilities.

Q: Did President Bush fail to appreciate the nuance you're talking about now?

A: I'm not a carbon copy of President Bush. And there are things I would do differently.

Source: GOP Iowa Straw Poll debate, Aug. 5, 2007

Obama on International Diplomacy

The UN has succeeded in avoiding a Third World War

With the advent of the nuclear age, it became clear to victor and vanquished alike that the world needed institutions to prevent another World War. And so, a quarter century after the US Senate rejected the League of Nations—an idea for which Woodrow Wilson received this Prize—America led the world in constructing an architecture to keep the peace: a Marshall Plan and a United Nations, mechanisms to govern the waging of war, treaties to protect human rights, prevent genocide, and restrict the most dangerous weapons.

In many ways, these efforts succeeded. Yes, terrible wars have been fought, and atrocities committed. But there has been no Third World War. The Cold War ended with jubilant crowds dismantling a wall. Billions have been lifted from poverty. The ideals of liberty, self-determination, equality and the rule of law have haltingly advanced. We are the heirs of the fortitude and foresight of generations past, and it is a legacy for which my own country is rightfully proud.

Source: Nobel Peace Prize acceptance speech in Oslo, Norway,
Dec 10, 2009

Romney on the Patriot Act

No Miranda rights for suicide bombers

Before we move away from this "No" epithet that the Democrats are fond of trying to apply to us, let's ask the Obama folks why they say no: no to a balanced budget, no to reforming entitlements, no to malpractice reform, no to missile defense in eastern Europe, no to prosecuting Khalid Sheikh Mohammed in a military tribunal.

Conservatism has had from its inception vigorously positive, intellectually rigorous agenda and thinking. That agenda should have, mind you, three pillars: strength in the economy, strength in our security and strength in our families.

We will strengthen our security by building missile defense, restoring our military might and standing by and strengthening our intelligence officers. Conservatives believe in providing constitutional rights to our citizens, not to enemy combatants like Khalid Sheikh Mohammed.

Not on our watch. A conversation with a would-be suicide bomber will not begin with the words, "You have the right to remain silent."

Source: Speech to Conservative Political Action Conference,
Feb 20, 2010

Obama on the Patriot Act

The politics of fear undermines basic civil liberties

What we cannot continue to do is operate as if we are the weakest nation in the world instead of the strongest one, because that's not who we are and that's not what the US has been about, historically. It is starting to warp our domestic policies, as well. We haven't even talked about civil liberties and the impact of that politics of fear— what that has done to us, in terms of undermining basic civil liberties in this country, what it has done in terms of our reputation around the world.

Source: Democratic debate at Drexel University, Oct. 30, 2007

FactCheck: Promised to repeal Patriot Act, then voted for it

Clinton took direct aim at Obama and connects fairly solidly: "You said you would vote against the Patriot Act; you came to the Senate, you voted for it." Clinton is correct to say that Obama opposed the Patriot Act during his run for the Senate. When it came time to reauthorize the law in 2005, though, Obama voted in favor of it. He started out opposing it: In Dec. 2005, Obama voted against ending debate—a position equivalent to declaring a lack of support for the measure. Then in February of that year, Obama said on the floor that he would support the Patriot Act's reauthorization. In March 2006, Obama both voted for cloture and for the Patriot Act reauthorization conference report. Clinton, by the way, followed exactly the same path on the 2005 bill, from speaking in opposition to voting for it.

Source: FactCheck.org on Facebook/WMUR-NH Democratic debate,
Jan. 5, 2008

Romney on Defense spending

Increase defense spending to at least 4% of GDP

In the face of Obama's approach and foreign policy agenda, we need to do several things. The first is fairly elementary: We should treat our allies like the allies they are. That means, for starters, not being harder on them, or demanding more from them, than we do from our adversaries.

To ensure that America remains safe and maintains its role as a defender of freedom, we also need to increase our defense spending to at least 4% of our GDP per year, including substantial and increasing support for missile defense. Under President Obama, our defense spending will decline as a share of our economy and of the federal budget. And it will fall far below what is required to meet our global commitments.

Source: No Apology, by Mitt Romney, p. 30-2, March 2, 2010

NOTES: America's GDP (Gross Domestic Product) stands at $14.7 trillion in 2012, according to *CIA World Factbook*. Gov. Romney's suggestion that we spend 4% of GDP on defense spending would mean a defense budget of $588 billion. President Obama's 2013 budget proposal includes $524 billion for defense, or 3.6% of GDP. Hence Romney would spend $64 billion more on defense than Obama in 2013.

Obama further proposes slowing the growth of defense spending in future years. Obama would increase the defense budget by 2% per year, while the CBO projects GDP to grow at about 3% per year. In 2017, Obama proposes $568 billion. Applying Romney's 4% target on 2017 GDP of about $17 trillion would mean $681 billion on defense. Hence Romney would spend $113 billion more on defense than Obama in 2017.

Obama on Defense spending

Reduce defense spending 1% in 2013; add 2% per year after

According to the first details of the Obama administration's fiscal 2013 defense budget, defense spending in 2013 would be reduced 1% from this year's initial $525 billion request before growing annually 1.8% in 2014, 2.3% in 2015, 1.9% in 2016, and 2.2% in 2017. The percentage increases are expressed in "nominal growth," not adjusted for inflation.

The administration plans $82 billion in funding for the Afghanistan and Iraq wars for 2013, according to the Office of Management and Budget (OMB). The basic defense-only "topline" numbers are currently projected at:

- $524 billion in 2013

- $533 billion in 2014

- $546 billion in 2015

- $556 billion in 2016

- $568 billion in 2017

The 2012-2021 defense plan calls for $5.652 trillion in spending. OMB calculated that the total Budget Control Act- mandated defense cut over those years is $488 billion—or about an 8.5% total decrease.

Source: Tony Capaccio in Bloomberg News, "First Budget Numbers,"
Jan. 11, 2012

Romney on Sources of Terrorism

To win the war on jihad,
we need friends in Muslim world

To win the war on jihad, we have to not only have a strong military of our own—and we need a stronger military—we also need to have strong friends around the world and help moderate Muslims reject the extreme. Because ultimately the only people who can finally defeat these radical Islamic jihadists are the Muslims themselves.

Source: 2007 GOP Iowa Straw Poll debate, Aug. 5, 2007

American resolve in Iraq counters jihad with fortitude

The jihadists' history with America justifies their confidence that we will abandon the fight. In 1983, jihadists attacked US marines in Lebanon—and we withdrew. The again in 1993, jihadists attacked US marines in Somalia—and we withdrew. In 2000, jihadists audaciously attacked the USS Cole, killing 17 American sailors, but we did nothing.

With all this history as a backdrop for their lectures to the young, jihadists have become quite confident in the knowledge that, time and again, we have underestimated their threat, their capacity to kill, and their steadfast resolve. This is a lesson they pass on to the young radicals in the making. Only in recent years has American resolve in Iraq and Afghanistan provided a counterexample of Western fortitude in the face of jihadist attacks.

Source: No Apology, by Mitt Romney, p. 71, March 2, 2010

Obama on Sources of Terrorism

Battling terrorism must go beyond belligerence vs. isolation

We know that the battle against terrorism is at once an armed struggle and a contest of ideas, that our long-term security depends on a judicious projection of military power and increased cooperation with other nations, and that addressing the problems of global poverty and failed states is vital to our nation's interests rather than just a matter of charity. But follow most of our foreign policy debates, and you might believe that we have only two choices—belligerence or isolationism.

Source: The Audacity of Hope, by Barack Obama, p. 23, Oct. 1, 2006

OpEd: Claims "poverty causes terrorism" but they're educated

Most suicide bombers are well-educated and have a generally higher socio-economic status. Nevertheless, the Obama administration continues to cling to the "poverty causes terrorism" theory because it supports the social work approach to national security that it favors.

If the Obama administration were to admit that Islamic terrorists are not motivated by poverty but rather by an evil ideology, that would require a paradigm shift in the way it approaches terrorism. They'd have to name the enemy, and acknowledge that military power rather than more anti-poverty programs must be the central means to fight and win.

Source: Leadership and Crisis, by Bobby Jindal, p.257–8, Nov. 15, 2010

Romney on Torture Policy

Best to not say whether waterboarding is torture or not

Q: In one of your recent debates, you refused to say whether waterboarding was torture. The director of national intelligence said flatly: "Whether it is torture by anybody else's definition, for me it would be torture." I wonder if that would influence you to conclude that waterboarding is torture, because you and McCain debated on that. McCain came down very, very firmly, saying waterboarding is torture.

A: You know, I just don't think it's productive for presidents to lay out a list of what is specifically referred to as torture. One of the reasons is that that term is used in the Geneva accord. And once you lay that list out, you are forever prohibiting the US from ever employing that technique, even in a circumstance where a city might be subject to a potential nuclear attack. And so we have found it wise, in the past, not to describe precisely the techniques of interrogation that are used here; also, so that people who are captured don't know what might be used against them.

Source: CNN Late Edition: 2008 presidential series with Wolf Blitzer,
Jan 13, 2008

Obama on Torture Policy

No torture; no renditions; no operating out of fear

We have to be clear and unequivocal. We do not torture, period. Our government does not torture. That should be our position. That will be my position as president. That includes renditions. We don't farm out torture. We don't subcontract torture. Torture does not end up yielding good information—most intelligence officers agree with that—but it is also important for our long-term security to send a message to the world that we will lead not just with our military might but we are going to lead with our values and our ideals. That we are not a nation that gives away our civil liberties simply because we're scared. We're always at our worst when we're fearful. Fear is a bad counsel and I want to operate out of hope and out of faith.

Source: Democratic Compassion Forum at Messiah College, April 13, 2008

Congress decides what constitutes torture, not president

Q: If Congress prohibits a specific interrogation technique, can the president instruct his subordinates to employ that technique despite the statute?

A: No. The President is not above the law, and not entitled to use techniques that Congress has specifically banned as torture. We must send a message to the world that America is a nation of laws, and a nation that stands against torture. As President I will abide by statutory prohibitions for all US Government personnel and contractors.

Source: Boston Globe questionnaire on Executive Power, Dec. 20, 2007

Romney on Guantanamo Prison

Closing Guantanamo leaves America
vulnerable to another 9/11

President Obama won the favor of liberal commentators by pledging what it calls reform in the treatment of terrorist detainees. He's also promised to close down Guantanamo, without giving the slightest indication of the next stop for the killers being held there now.

But here's the problem. That is the very kind of thinking that left America vulnerable to the attacks of September 11th.

This is not a law enforcement problem. It is the gravest matter of national security, with thousands if not millions of lives in the balance. The jihadists are still at war with America. Our government has no greater duty than a vigilant defense, and no greater cause than victory for America and for freedom.

Gestures that communicate a lack of resolve only embolden America's adversaries. With Iran seeking nuclear weapons, with North Korea already nuclear and selling its technology to the Syrians, it is essential that we construct a missile defense, now.

Source: Speech to Conservative Political Action Conference,
Feb. 27, 2009

Obama on Guantanamo Prison

OpEd: Promised to close Guantanamo but it's still open

The litany of broken Obama promises is amazing:

He promised to get us out of Iraq. But we're still there.

He promised cap and trade. But he hasn't produced.

He said he'd bring down the deficit. But he's tripled it.

He promised to close Guantanamo. But it's still open for business.

He said he'd fix Social Security. But he hasn't touched it.

You may disagree with many of these promises. You're probably glad they failed. But don't let that stop you from using them to defeat Obama.

Source: Take Back America, by Dick Morris, p.262, April 13, 2010

Promises to close Guantanamo & treat prisoners as POWs

The Bush administration argued that because [prisoners at Guantanamo] are not state-sponsored, they are not entitled to the usual protections of the Geneva Convention.

President Barack Obama will close the detention facility at Guantanamo Bay and remove the "unlawful enemy combatants" status from those detained. Both charges will accelerate resolution of the basic questions that remain: What is the adjudication process and what is the standard against which their actions will be measured to justify release?

Source: The Test of our Times, by Tom Ridge, p.144-5, Sept. 1, 2009

Romney on Afghanistan War

Stay in Afghanistan until our generals say to leave

Q: Osama bin Laden is dead. We've been in Afghanistan for ten years. Isn't it time to bring our combat troops home from Afghanistan?

ROMNEY: It's time for us to bring our troops home as soon as we possibly can, consistent with the word that comes to our generals that we can hand the country over to the Afghan military to defend themselves from the Taliban. I think we've learned some important lessons in our experience in Afghanistan. I want those troops to come home based upon not politics, not based upon economics, but instead based upon the conditions on the ground determined by the generals. But I also think we've learned that our troops shouldn't go off and try and fight a war of independence for another nation. Only the Afghanis can win Afghanistan's independence from the Taliban.

Q: Congressman Paul, do you agree with that decision?

PAUL: Not quite. I make the decisions. I tell the generals what to do. I'd bring them home as quickly as possible.

Source: 2011 GOP primary debate in Manchester NH, June 13, 2011

Obama on Afghanistan War

Troops will begin to exit Afghanistan in July 2011

In Afghanistan, we're increasing our troops, and training Afghan security forces so they can begin to take the lead in July of 2011, and our troops can begin to come home. We will reward good governance, work to reduce corruption, and support the rights of all Afghans—men and women alike. We're joined by allies and partners who have increased their own commitments. There will be difficult days ahead. But I am absolutely confident we will succeed.

Source: 2010 State of the Union Address, Jan. 27, 2010

We've taken the fight to al Qaeda in Afghanistan, until July 2011

As we speak, al Qaeda and their affiliates continue to plan attacks against us. Thanks to our intelligence and law enforcement professionals, we're disrupting plots and securing our cities and skies. We've also taken the fight to al Qaeda and their allies abroad. In Afghanistan, our troops have taken Taliban strongholds and trained Afghan security forces. Our purpose is clear: By preventing the Taliban from reestablishing a stranglehold over the Afghan people, we will deny al Qaeda the safe haven that served as a launching pad for 9/11.

We are strengthening the capacity of the Afghan people and building an enduring partnership with them. This year, we will work with nearly 50 countries to begin a transition to an Afghan lead. And this July, we will begin to bring our troops home.

Source: 2011 State of the Union Address, Jan. 26, 2011

Book Reviews

OnTheIssues excerpts political books and debates as the primary source of the materials in this book. Following are several book reviews, plus links online to additional books and debates cited in this book.

Book reviews:

Additional book excerpts online:

Game Change, by Heilemann and Halperin (2010)
    www.OnTheIssues.org/Game_Change.htm

What Obama Means, by Jabari Asim (2009)
    www.OnTheIssues.org/Obama_Means.htm

The Faith of Barack Obama, by Stephen Mansfield (2008)
    www.OnTheIssues.org/*Faith_Obama.htm*

A Mormon in the White House?, by Hugh Hewitt (2007)
    www.OnTheIssues.org/Mormon_White_House.htm

The Man, His Values & His Vision, by Turner & Field (2007)
    www.OnTheIssues.org/Man_Values_Vision.htm

Book Review: *Turnaround:*
Crisis, Leadership, and the Olympic Games by Gov. Mitt Romney (June 15, 2004)

This book is about Mitt Romney's experience as the chairman of the Salt Lake Organizing Committee (SLOC), which ran the Salt Lake City Winter Olympic Games in 2002. Some of Romney's comments in the book hail back to his time at Bain Capital, or forward to his time as Governor of Massachusetts. But mostly it's about SLOC, so most of our excerpts are about the principles & values he developed and/or describes from there.

Romney is widely credited with "turning around" the Olympics, after a series of scandals within SLOC involving corruption and bad financial planning. Romney overcame both problems, and pulled off a successful Olympics, which was viewed as having recovered the integrity of the Games, while also turning a profit.

Romney's performance in the Olympics was exemplary and outstandingly positive. However, he claims he never thought about the political implications of running the Olympics; and he claims he never considered running for Governor while at the Olympics. I don't believe that for one second. Romney ran for Senate against Ted Kennedy in the 1990s, and made a decent showing against the single most entrenched incumbent in the Senate. Everyone in Massachusetts politics, including myself, always assumed Romney would run for office again, and fully expected him to segue from the Olympics to a gubernatorial run. If Romney was surprised by that turn of events, he was the only one!

Romney, in effect, rode the coattails of his Olympic turnaround to victory in the Massachusetts gubernatorial election of 2002. There was no gap between the two—Romney flew back from Utah and immediately entered the gubernatorial race. Similarly, there was no gap after Romney retired from the Governor's position—he announced for President the day after the inauguration of Deval Patrick, his successor. So Romney is still, in effect, riding the coattails of the Olympics in the presidential race.

P.S. Full disclosure: I worked as a senior (paid) staffer for the Robert Reich for Governor campaign, which was a Democratic campaign in the primary when Romney was the only Republican candidate. After Reich's loss in the primary, I volunteered with the Shannon O'Brien campaign, which directly ran against Romney in the general election.

Book review written May 2011;
full excerpts available online at:
www.ontheissues.org/No_Apology.htm

Book Review: *No Apology:*
The Case for American Greatness
by Gov. Mitt Romney (March 2, 2010)

This book, published in 2010, outlines Mitt Romney's case against Obama for the 2012 election. Its title makes Romney's case that Obama is an apologist for America (pp.24-33) whereas Romney would instead "proudly defend her." If the title sounds arrogant, that too is Romney's intent: he claims that Obama is too weak in missile defense (p. 18); in defense spending (p. 31); in the War on Terror (p. 64); and in just about everything.

While this book focuses heavily on foreign policy and military issues, Romney also makes the domestic case against Obama. Romney reinforces his conservative credentials against abortion (p. 265) and against gay marriage (p. 269), since those credentials need substantial reinforcement in the view of many hard-line conservatives (Romney ran against Ted Kennedy for the Massachusetts Senate seat in 1994 as a pro-gay, pro-choice Republican).

But mostly Romney focuses on healthcare. And mostly he focuses on how RomneyCare (the Massachusetts healthcare plan initiated by Romney as Governor) is not the same as ObamaCare (p. 176). Mostly

Romney's opponents will focus on how ObamaCare is based heavily on RomneyCare: the 2012 Republican primary voters will have to decide which view prevails.

On the question of whether Romney is running in 2012, this book answers unambiguously "Yes." Romney never actually SAYS that, of course. But candidates never do. The book's purpose is to establish Romney as sharing core conservative values, which he will need to win the primary election. And the book's other purpose is to establish Romney's line of attack against Obama, which he will need to win the general election. In summary, this book outlines Romney's campaign plans for 2012.

Book review written May 2011;
full excerpts available online at:
www.ontheissues.org/No_Apology.htm

Book Review:
Dreams from My Father:
A Story of Race and Inheritance
by Barack Obama (August 1996)

This is the book to read if you want to understand Obama's personal background and how it forms his character. It was written while he was still only an obscure State Senator—written in his spare time, without a ghost writer, while struggling to make ends meet on a state senator's salary. Therefore it is an honest portrait, made before Obama even intended to run for US Senate, much less for President.

Here I'll discuss one aspect of Obama's background, which is his internationalism. I'm writing this shortly after Obama returned from his "campaign trip" abroad, which included fact-finding in Iraq and drawing a crowd of 200,000 fans in Germany. While the mainstream press was overwhelmingly enamored with Obama on that trip, it has become clear upon Obama's return that the voting public has not responded nearly as positively. Obama's popularity abroad relates to Obama's international upbringing, as outlined in this book.

Obama spent several years of his childhood living abroad—four years in Indonesia. In addition, he maintains contact with his paternal family in Kenya (where, during his 2007 visit, he also was greeted as a hero). And his birthplace and family home is Hawaii, arguably the most international of the fifty states.

The question for the presidential race is this: Does Obama's personal experience living abroad count as foreign policy expertise? I would say Yes; but the voting public has declared No. In other words, McCain's argument that Obama has no foreign policy expertise has prevailed.

I would say Yes, because I personally have a similar experience as Obama, and I consider that a valid basis for claiming foreign policy expertise. I've resided in Denmark, Hong Kong, and Israel, for 6 to 12 months each; I've traveled to more than 40 countries and spent a total of about 4 or 5 years abroad; I've been in relationships with women living in England, Denmark, Hong Kong, and Pakistan. I do consider that I have substantial foreign policy expertise, entirely on the basis of that personal experience.

To illustrate why that qualifies me as a foreign policy expert, I'll relate my experience in a class on foreign policy at the Master's degree level at Harvard University in the early 1990s. I attended an introductory class on foreign policy with the intent of concentrating in that field. But I found that my fellow students had relatively little knowledge of world politics—despite that most had just graduated from foreign policy undergraduate institutions. For example, we discussed Japan's relations with its neighbors, and my fellow students suggested that Japan should be creating a trading bloc (like ASEAN or NAFTA) with China, Korea, and Russia, its nearest neighbors. It was obvious to me that Japan could never do such a thing, because the Koreans await an apology for WWII enslavement; the Chinese await reparations for the "Rape of Nanjing"; and the Russians await resolution of the disputed Kuril Islands. I knew those things first-hand from Japanese co-workers in Hong Kong, who were reluctant to visit those areas with me. My classmates knew little about those sort of "facts on the ground," and I ended up switching my field of concentration to the more experience-oriented "International Development."

Obama is an internationalist. That means, not only does he believe in globalization as an economic and military policy, but he is accustomed to presenting himself abroad as an American—which most Americans are not. America is an isolated country—unless we go out of our way to travel abroad and experience it intimately, we don't participate in the rest of the world. The consequence of that isolation is that we don't deeply understand foreigners' points of view. Internationalist Americans DO understand foreigners—and foreigners are well-aware of distinguishing internationalist Americans from our more isolated brethren. Obama's massive crowd of supporters in Germany was an acknowledgement from the Germans that they recognize Obama as an internationalist. The press' enthrallment with Obama on his foreign trip was because the press saw that other foreigners recognized that too, and assumed it would translate to popularity at home.

But most Americans are not internationalists. The press got it wrong because they only reported on what foreigners felt—while foreigners don't vote in the US presidential election. Obama thought he would be seen on this trip as Presidential—but in fact his popularity abroad was seen as just another way in which Obama differs from most Americans, because most Americans are not internationalist. Hence Obama's trip abroad was seen as elitist by most American voters—not as evidence of foreign policy expertise, even though it *was* seen that way abroad.

I consider myself an internationalist too. But I acknowledge that I'm in a small minority among my countrymen. My internationalist background certainly colors all of my politics—but usually I shut up about the origins of my political philosophy, because I don't want to be seen as elitist.

How does all that affect the presidential election? Well, Obama better shut up about his internationalism too, or he'll alienate most Americans by seeming elitist. And, although any internationalist would certainly grant Obama the lead over McCain in relevant foreign policy expertise, the American voting public will not. Therefore Obama needs to pick a Vice President who has more conventional foreign policy expertise, to counter McCain's attacks on this front.

Book review written Aug. 2008;
full excerpts available online at:
www.ontheissues.org/Dreams_From_My_Father.htm

Book Review:
The Audacity of Hope:
Thoughts on Reclaiming
the American Dream
by Barack Obama (Oct. 2006)

Who is the audience for this book? Most people buy it to keep it on their coffeetable to start conversations—the typical voter would not read it through. Most political analysts know everything that's in here already—there are no daring new policies nor deep personal revelations. I've concluded that the intended audience is the excerpter—people like me. This book got excerpted in Time magazine, for example, and Obama got a big cover spread, with a presidential headline. The Time excerpts were pleasant to read—a little uplift for a few pages. But the book is just so chock-full of respectfulness and understanding and consensus-building and bipartisanship that no excerpter can find anything *but* uplift in any excerpt (including me).

So my conclusion is that the book is *intended* for that purpose—a successful attempt to get Obama into the national spotlight by writing a political tome that everyone will like and few will actually read through. This book contains nothing but numerous uplifting anecdotes of building consensus based on understanding one's opponents' point of view, of bipartisanship based on mutual respect. Reading an excerpt or two fills one with an uplifting feeling. Reading the original in its entirety, however, feels like slogging through uplifting anecdote after uplifting anecdote, to the point where it feels formulaically forced. The formula goes like this for every issue: "The proponents believe X. The opponents believe Y. I tend to lean toward the proponents' views, but I have great respect for the opponents, and we should work together on consensus solutions." I imagine that Obama met with his ghostwriter and outlined his issue stances, then told the ghostwriter to frame each one in a context of that sort of bipartisan respect.

Overall, of course, this is exactly the sort of book needed for the presidential trail. Having the book on coffeetables across America, despite being unread, means Barack's smiling face is in people's living rooms and he's in people's conversations. Having uplifting anecdotes excerpted in Time and OnTheIssues means people will read about their favorite topic, be uplifted, and repeat the anecdote to their fellow voters. It doesn't matter that the *same* formula is used for *every* issue—people aren't interested in *every* issue, just their favorite ones. But if you want to get to know Obama, read instead Dreams From My Father, which is indeed a revealing biography and a deep look at his compelling personal story. This book is written instead for the campaign trail.

I do have a fantasy about how Obama came up with the title (because people like Obama hire people like me to come up with titles like "The Audacity of Hope"). I imagine that Obama wants to elicit a subconscious connection with Howard Dean—who is characterized by his audacious campaign style—and simultaneously elicit a subconscious connection with Bill Clinton—whose book titles often include his hometown of Hope, Arkansas, as in Between Hope and History. Obama's title hence attempts to elicit a subconscious feeling that "Obama has the audacity of Dean, but with Clinton's chances of success." Maybe I'm reading too much subconsciousness into it—but it's people like me who write these titles, so who knows.

Summer 2008 postscript: Indeed my title theory was a fantasy— the title came from a sermon given by the now-famous Rev. Jeremiah Wright.

Book review written May 2007;
full excerpts available online at:
www.ontheissues.org/Audacity_of_Hope.htm

Book Review:
Obama's Challenge:
America's Economic Crisis and the
Power of a Transformative Presidency,
by Robert Kuttner (Aug. 25, 2008)

We expected this book to be a perceptive analysis of the Obama campaign, since it won a prize (the Sidney Hillman Award), and since the author, Robert Kuttner, co-founded "The American Prospect," a well-respected liberal publication. Alas, the author is partisan rather than perceptive, and the book is fatally tainted by the author's biases. Some partisanship, and some punditry, are forgivable. But the fatal taint comes from the unforgivable—and politically inaccurate— partisanship of mischaracterizing "progressives" vs. "liberals."

Kuttner can be forgiven for some partisanship, since he's a well-known as a liberal Democrat. Perceptive readers recognize his partisanship in his statement describing Obama's activist use of government: "Which party is more likely to manage government in a way that doesn't arbitrarily diminish rights?" (p. 90). Well, which rights? Kuttner means gay rights, civil rights, labor rights, and so on. But a conservative could answer, "The GOP, of course, is less likely to diminish gun rights, free trade rights, and the right to life." After statements like Kuttner's above, readers acknowledge that Kuttner is writing an opinion piece, not an analysis piece, and thereafter read the book cautiously, differentiating Kuttner's opinions from analysis about Obama.

Kuttner can also be forgiven for some punditry, since he has earned his place as a pundit. He wrote this book during the 2008 election, and published it in August 2008, as "a citizen's open letter" to the Obama campaign. Kuttner admits his presumptuousness in predicting that Obama will win the election three months hence; readers acknowledge Kuttner's presumptuousness in thinking that the Obama campaign would care about his "open letter." After all, it's also an "open letter" to his fellow citizens, about how Obama would be a "transformative president" (that's Kuttner's subtitle. He means Obama will permanently change America, as did Abraham Lincoln, FDR, and Ronald Reagan).

But Kuttner cannot be forgiven for mischaracterizing the term "progressive." That term defined the difference between Obama (a progressive) and Hillary Clinton (a liberal) during the 2008 primary, so it is core to the election. Kuttner does identify Obama as a progressive, but also identifies as progressives LBJ, Hillary, John Edwards, and others. Kuttner writes in chapter one, "Progressives who backed Obama rather than John Edwards or Hillary Clinton for the Democratic nomination gave Obama a pass on some of the issues." (pp. 7-8). That statement is politically inaccurate twice. Where I come from, no progressives backed John Edwards nor Hillary Clinton. I know many, many progressives—they all backed Obama, or Dennis Kucinich, or maybe Mike Gravel. And I know many, many liberals—they all backed John Edwards or Hillary Clinton. It was a clean split, where I come from—and that's also where Kuttner comes from, since we both live in the Boston area. Kuttner must be well-aware of that split, but he misleads his readers by conflating the two political philosophies.

The second inaccuracy in that same statement is that progressives gave Obama a pass on some issues. Kuttner thinks like a liberal, and that statement only makes sense from a liberal perspective, where the focus is on economic issues (labor rights, appropriate taxation, protecting Social Security). Progressives instead focus on social issues (gay rights, protesting and ending the Iraq war, civil rights). Progressives backed Obama because he matched their views and their focus on social issues; liberals backed Hillary and Edwards on the same grounds for economic issues. Progressives would not give a pass to Hillary or Edwards for their pro-Iraq war votes because that's a core part of the progressive agenda.

That distinction between economic issues and social issues is the focal distinction of this website—see our "VoteMatch Quiz" for details. That same distinction differentiated Obama from Hillary, and differentiates the two factions of the Democratic Party, the progressives vs. the liberals. And that same distinction applies to the Republican

Party too—its current three factions differ in their social vs. economic focus:

- Christian conservatives focus on social issues (on the opposite side from progressives)

- Tea Party conservatives focus on economic issues (on the opposite side from liberals)

- Libertarians focus on both issues at once (on the opposite side from populists, but these groups aren't relevant to this discussion).

Kuttner's truly unforgivable partisanship comes from mischaracterizing the 2006 Senate election. This statement goes beyond partisan punditry into the realm of factual misrepresentation: "All six of the Democrats who took back Republican senate seats in 2006 ran as resolute progressives." (p. 112) Huh?!? Let's take a look at the six Democrats Kuttner refers to:

- Sherrod Brown (D, OH) and Sheldon Whitehouse (D, RI) are indeed resolute progressives.

- Claire McCaskill (D, MO) is best described as a moderate, not a "resolute progressive," but the other three should not even be described as *any* kind of progressive:

- Jim Webb (D, VA) is pro-gun;

- Jon Tester (D, MT) is pro-gun and pro-Drug War;

- Bob Casey (D, PA) is pro-gun; pro-life; pro-death penalty; pro-Patriot Act; and more!

Sen. Casey, in particular, ran his campaign clearly in the populist center politically—no one during the campaign would have described him as a progressive, and certainly no one looking at his voting record afterwards would! So what could Kuttner possibly mean? Well, look at the list above, and all are social issues—ones that matter to progressives. All six of the new Senators toe the line on the Democratic view of economic issues—ones that matter to liberals.

It's ok that Kuttner is a liberal. But he pretends to be a progressive. And he adds confusion to the debate between progressives and liberals, the ongoing central debate of the Democratic Party. Readers need to be careful in this book to interpret Kuttner's use of the term "progressive" because he often means "liberal." His other analysis might be interesting; but his opinions on progressivism are just factually erroneous.

Book review written Jan. 2011;
full excerpts available online at:
www.ontheissues.org/Obama_Challenge.htm

Romney vs. Obama on VoteMatch

VoteMatch is our 20-question quiz which summarizes the candidate's views on the controversial issues of the day.

VoteMatch Social Issues

	Mitt Romney	Barack Obama
Abortion is a woman's right	opposes	strongly favors
Require companies to hire more women & minorities	strongly favors	strongly favors
Same-sex domestic partnership benefits	opposes	favors
Teacher-led prayer in public schools	strongly favors	opposes
Parents choose schools via vouchers	strongly favors	favors

VoteMatch Domestic Issues

	Mitt Romney	Barack Obama
More federal funding for health coverage	neutral	strongly favors
Death Penalty	strongly favors	opposes
Mandatory Three Strikes sentencing laws	strongly favors	opposes
Absolute right to gun ownership	opposes	opposes
Drug use is immoral: enforce laws against it	strongly favors	opposes

VoteMatch Economic Issues

	Mitt Romney	Barack Obama
Privatize Social Security	strongly favors	strongly opposes
Make taxes more progressive	strongly opposes	strongly favors
Stricter limits on political campaign funds	opposes	strongly favors
Allow churches to provide welfare services	favors	favors
Replace coal & oil with alternatives	opposes	strongly favors

VoteMatch International Issues

	Mitt Romney	Barack Obama
Illegal immigrants earn citizenship	opposes	favors
Support & expand free trade	neutral	opposes
The Patriot Act harms civil liberties	strongly opposes	strongly favors
Expand the armed forces	strongly favors	favors
US out of Iraq and Afghanistan	strongly opposes	favors

In our online quiz, you fill in your answers for these 20 questions, and we match you against all the candidates. Please see:

http://quiz.ontheissues.org/

Afterword

We hope that this book encourages you, as voters, to make your decisions based on the issues. We recognize the reality of American politics: voters make their decisions based primarily on whether they like the candidates. Accordingly, our goal is to get voters to compare their issue preferences in comparison to candidate issue stances when considering which candidates to like.

We intentionally omitted from this book any biographical background on Gov. Romney and President Obama. Details of their birthplaces and religious affiliations—and minutiae of every other personal detail—are readily available in the mainstream media. Their issue stances are more challenging for voters to find.

Why does the mainstream media fail at this important function? Because they are "news" organizations which are poorly suited to covering political campaigns. "News" implies reporting on what is "new": Obama's stance on criminal sentencing has not changed since 1998, and Romney's stance on welfare-to-work has not changed since 1994, so there's nothing in the news about those issues. But if you are impassioned about Three Strikes, or if you vote based on welfare policy, then you can't rely on the news media for those non-newsworthy issues. And that's where we come in.

This book represents an archive of where these two candidates stand on the key issues of our time. We don't consider whether candidates' issue stances are new—just what they say on each issue. That often requires a lot of digging on our part—we have a team of researchers to do that, but we invite you to volunteer any issue stances that we don't cover.

Our online website www.ontheissues.org covers many more issues than can fit in any book: many more stances from Barack Obama and Mitt Romney, as well as all of the other 2012 candidates, Governors, Senators, and House members. We score each candidate on a 20-question quiz called "VoteMatch." A representation of the VoteMatch quiz results for the presidential contenders appears on the back cover of this book. The mainstream media interpret candidates using a one-dimensional "right-left" analysis. That simplistic analysis comes to nonsensical conclusions like calling Ron Paul "extreme right-wing" even though he opposes the Iraq War; opposes the Patriot Act; supports drug legalization; and supports same-sex domestic partnership benefits.

We find our two-dimensional analysis to be more accurate in differentiating candidates than that traditional one-dimensional analysis. We don't claim that our method is perfect—just superior to the simplistic mainstream media. VoteMatch uses a Social Issues dimension plus an Economic Issues dimension; we interpret candidates based on whether they believe in government involvement in either or both of those dimensions. Using the two-dimensional analysis differentiates five classes of political beliefs:

1. *Libertarian:*
   No government involvement in social issues
   No government involvement in economic issues

2. *Conservative:*
   Government involvement in social issues
   No government involvement in economic issues

3. *Liberal:*
   No government involvement in social issues
   Government involvement in economic issues

4. *Populist:*
   Government involvement in social issues
   Government involvement in economic issues

5. *Centrist:*
   Some government involvement in social issues
   Some government involvement in economic issues

Most importantly, you can answer the same 20 questions and see *your* political label and how the candidates match up with *you*. We invite you to try the VoteMatch quiz at:

http://quiz.ontheissues.org

Other Books in This Series

- Rick Perry vs. Mitt Romney On The Issues

- Sarah Palin vs. Michele Bachmann On The Issues

- Mitt Romney vs. Newt Gingrich On The Issues

- Rick Santorum vs. Mitt Romney On The Issues

- Ron Paul vs. Barack Obama On The Issues

About the Author

Jesse Gordon has been the editor-in-chief of OnTheIssues.org since its formation in 1999. His passion revolves around providing issue-based coverage on political races, to combat the mainstream media's growing lack of such coverage.

Mr. Gordon holds a Master's degree in Public Policy from Harvard University's Kennedy School of Government. He and the website OnTheIssues.org are based in Cambridge, Massachusetts. He resides with his fiancée, Kathleen; his son Julien; Kathleen's son Derek; their cat Chanel; and six fish with whom Chanel is obsessed.

Mr. Gordon replies to email personally, at jesse@ontheissues.org—whether to suggest improvements to the website or to order one of the other books above.